P9-EDJ-607

HYMNS WE LOVE

HYMNS WE LOVE

Stories of the
Hundred Most Popular Hymns

by

ARTHUR TEMPLE

LUTTERWORTH PRESS
LONDON

Printed in Great Britain by Latimer Trend & Co. Ltd.
Plymouth

FOREWORD

THIS book grew out of correspondence with hymn-lovers in Australia, Canada, the United States of America and in Britain.

The idea was to discover which hymns, out of the multitude available, were the popular choices of the people in the English speaking countries. That is more easily discoverable nowadays because of radio and television hymn services where choices of hymns are sent in by post, or telephone, or are made by local community hymn-singing groups.

A hundred hymns emerged from the choosing and sifting and their stories are told here. Some of the choices hymnologists would not put amongst the great hymns of Christendom, and some of the hymns do not find a place in the various hymn-books of the churches. But they have their place nevertheless in the religious life of great numbers of people.

A brief commentary is added to a hymn in some instances, for a hymn is often an essay in compressed theology. One of the dangers of hymn-singing is an unintelligent warbling of lines and verses whose meaning is complicated and obscure. A hymn-writer will often wrap a whole library of theology into a few lines, and the hymn-singer may be in high danger of mere word mumbling.

A thorough commentary on the "hundred hymns" would, of course, require a large volume. But on the whole the "hundred hymns" speak for themselves largely because they are hymns about the great central beliefs of the Christian faith, and in that sense they are a book of apologetics, a book of prayer as well as a collection of hymns.

Acknowledgment with thanks is given to officials of the British Broadcasting Corporation, the Australian Broadcasting Commission, the Canadian Broadcasting Corporation, and the National Broadcasting Company of America, who supplied information from their records; to the Rodeheaver Co. for permission to quote from *The Old Rugged Cross*, by G. Bennard (copyright 1941, renewal The Rodeheaver Co., owner, Winona Lake, Ind., U.S.A.) and from *In the Garden*, by C. A. Miles (copyright 1940, renewal The Rodeheaver Co., owner); to John Murray, Ltd., for the quotation from the *Founder's Day Hymn for King Henry VI*, by A. C. Ainger; to Miss Erica Oxenham for the verse quoted from *In Christ there is no East or West*, taken from *Bees in Amber*, by John Oxenham; to J. Curwen and Sons for the verses quoted from *Onward Christian Soldiers* and *Now the Day is Over*, by S. Baring-Gould; and to the Oxford University Press for permission to quote from *O God of Earth and Altar*, by G. K. Chesterton. If in quoting from hymns the author has unwittingly infringed copyright he offers his apologies in advance. Wherever possible, permission for quotations has been obtained. Criticism and suggestions were also most helpfully given by Brigadier Avery of the Salvation Army, the Rev. Frank Colquhoun, Dr. Alexander MacMillan of Toronto, and Dr. Erik Routley. Correspondence on the hymns will be welcomed by the author c/o Lutterworth Press, 4 Bouverie Street, London, E.C.4.

CONTENTS

7

THE HYMNS CHOSEN

In his great *Dictionary of Hymnology* John Julian estimated that there were more than 400,000 Christian hymns in two hundred languages of the world. That was at the beginning of the twentieth century.

How many more hymns have been written since then and brought into the various hymn-books of the world no one knows. It is probably much nearer the million mark, a vast gathering of poetry, rhymes and tunes celebrating the verities of the Christian Faith.

Such a mass of hymns demands a selection. That is why there has been an outpouring of hundreds of collections of hymns, not all of them, as in recent years, associated with the chief denominations but hymn-books which often were personal and meant for the use of small groups of people.

There was a time in Britain, at the beginning of the nineteenth century, when many of the chief towns had their representative collections of hymns. Thomas Cotterill of Sheffield, for instance, was an adept at collecting hymns, and roused his congregation at St. Paul's, Sheffield, to wrath in 1819 when he tried to force on it a large and expensive new edition. Eventually the Archbishop of York had to arbitrate, and neatly suggested that the book should be dedicated to him, which gave it an even bigger sales fillip in the north of England.

In the United States too about the same time hymn-books were beginning to appear: they were in the wake of the great victory for hymn-writing which Isaac Watts achieved when he led English speaking people away from the dour solemnities of psalm chanting. One edition of Watts' psalms and hymns edited by the famous Timothy Dwight of Yale was dubbed *Dwight's Watts*, and a rival, which had "select harmonies", was christened *Watts and Select*.

English speaking people everywhere seem to enjoy the fun of collecting hymns, arranging them in various orders, printing them and selling them. It is a happy field of private enterprise. Like hymn-writing itself, a hymn-book nearly always displays the faith and theology of its editor. For instance in Britain it does not take a theologian alone to discover the differing emphases between *The English Hymnal* and *Songs of Praise*, or between the British *Methodist Hymn Book* and the American *Pilgrim Hymnal*.

I once heard a wise man of religion say that "a good hymn-book is the prayer-book of the ordinary man". Any of the recent collections of hymns in the English speaking world to-day may be taken as an example of this, for those who sing in English are probably better provided with sound stuff to sing than at any time in the history of hymn-singing. For most of the great Christian churches have now re-edited their hymn-books—a task which needs to be done every twenty or thirty years in order that each generation shall sing what it believes, rather than hum the inherited beliefs of its grandfathers.

Looking down the contents of one of them, *Congregational Praise* for the Congregationalists of Britain, I see an outline of the Christian Faith and a Commentary on it. It runs like this:

THE ETERNAL FATHER
THE LORD JESUS CHRIST
THE HOLY SPIRIT
THE TRINITY
THE HOLY SCRIPTURES
THE CHURCH
THE LIFE OF DISCIPLESHIP

Over 500 hymns comprise the heart of the book, and they preserve the Christian faith in as lively and as meaningful a way as could be devised. That is why hymn-singing is not just poor poetry set to third-rate music. Much of it looks and sounds like that, but the singer who sings with belief in his heart knows otherwise.

Each of the sections I have mentioned has at least one peerless verse which speaks for all time, verses which the English hymn-singing world puts amongst the immortals.

> I'll praise my Maker while I've breath,
>   And when my voice is lost in death
>   Praise shall employ my nobler powers:
> My days of praise shall ne'er be past,
> While life and thought and being last,
>   Or immortality endures.

Isaac Watts never wrote a finer verse of praise, and praise is the first thing to look for in any hymn-book. How well the singer in English is provided for!

So it is with the trumpet sound of Edward Perronet's verse,

> All hail the power of Jesu's Name,
>   Let angels prostrate fall;
> Bring forth the royal diadem
>   To crown Him Lord of all.

Then the book opens out into the practices and

proclamations of Christianity, and becomes a companion fit to go with the Bible and Anglican Prayer Book as a working liturgy for life,

> Holy Spirit, truth divine,
> Dawn upon this soul of mine;
> Word of God, and inward light,
> Wake my spirit, clear my sight.

Samuel Longfellow's hymn gives him a place in the affection of English speaking people as much as anything his brother the poet wrote. Another debt to the United States is Mary Lathbury's

> Break Thou the bread of life,
> Dear Lord, to me,
> As Thou didst break the loaves
> Beside the sea.

Mary Lathbury also wrote that popular evening hymn *Day is dying in the west* but her "hymn to the Scriptures" is her real memorial. From the Scriptures we move to the church,

> Glorious things of thee are spoken,
> Zion, city of our God;
> He, whose word cannot be broken,
> Formed thee for His own abode:
> On the Rock of Ages founded,
> What can shake thy sure repose?
> With salvation's walls surrounded,
> Thou mayst smile at all thy foes.

John Newton stands amongst the elect group of hymn-writers who with his friend William Cowper helped to shape the English hymn tradition. Cowper comes most aptly in the "Life of Discipleship" section of the hymnbook I have opened,

Hark, my soul! it is the Lord:
  'Tis thy Saviour, hear His word;
Jesus speaks, and speaks to thee,
  "Say, poor sinner, lov'st thou Me?"

A more robust summons to the Christian life is in William Pierson Merrill's hymn which he wrote out of the life of busy pastorates in Philadelphia, Chicago and New York,

Rise up, O men of God!
  Have done with lesser things;
Give heart and soul and mind and strength
  To serve the King of Kings.

There, briefly, is the layout of belief as a modern hymn-book sees it. Not all the hymns, however, in this 500 would be called popular, because no hymn-book could live long on popular hymns alone.

A hymn-book is primarily a book of worship, and only incidentally a collection of hymns we like to sing. But at the same time someone, or a group of people, has to make the choice. That is what makes hymn choosing a fascinating occupation which no group of people finally agree about, and now that community singing, through radio and television, gives millions the chance to choose it is all the more fascinating. If Watts and Wesley taught the English speaking world to sing hymns, then radio and television have completed their task, for hymns ride triumphantly over the air, and as most of them, in programmes like the B.B.C.'s "Sunday Half-Hour", are popular choices there is to-day a fairly reliable guide to what hymns people like, and how often they want to sing them.

I

"Listening in" to hymn-singing draws its tens of millions in Britain, the United States and Australia and

Canada, but the basic supply of hymns that are chosen for the air—through individual clergymen, church congregations, choirs and singing groups—is much smaller than is usually supposed.

The reservoir of half a million hymns—or whatever the number is—is not taxed to any limit at all. Indeed any parson or choirmaster knows what a hard job it is to get a congregation going on a new hymn. We are rightly conservative about what hymns we sing because the hymns of our affection are usually the ones which speak to the great doctrines of the faith, and like a classic piece of Scripture we are suspicious of substitutes.

Looking down an average choice of a B.B.C. "Sunday Half-Hour" from the Parish Church of St. James the Great, Lower Gornal, I see the following hymns were sung from that Staffordshire country church:

> Thou didst leave thy throne
> Spirit Divine attend our prayers
> Jesus calls us
> Breathe on me, Breath of God
> Take my life and let it be
> O for a heart to praise my God
> Stand up and bless the Lord
> O Jesu, bless our homes

The last hymn is probably the only one that a hardened hymn-singer and listener would be unfamiliar with.

From the "land of song" at Siloh Welsh Presbyterian Church, Aberystwyth, comes this list of choices even more familiar, except perhaps the fifth choice,

> Praise, my soul, the king of heaven
> All creatures of our God and King
> For all the saints

14

All hail the power of Jesu's name
Come ye faithful raise the anthem
Praise the Lord ye heavens adore him

Another group of choices from Wrexham includes a whole row of favourites,

O for a thousand tongues
All hail the power of Jesu's name
Praise my soul the king of heaven
Jesus, lover of my soul
O come, O come, Emmanuel
Who is on the Lord's side
The Lord's my shepherd
The day thou gavest

Popular radio choices run to the old and familiar, the spacious hymns with the broad, deep themes of faith and experience, and that is true for most of the English speaking world.

In looking at an analysis of the B.B.C.'s "Sunday Half-Hour" over a period of two years one is struck by the fact that the hymns asked for more than four times during that period number only forty-eight. They might be called the "first favourites" because Australian and Canadian hymn-singers, on the evidence of the Australian Broadcasting Commission and the Canadian Broadcasting Corporation, range themselves roughly round the same list and—with some sharper variations—so does the United States. Within the first forty-eight there are some revealing victories for the favourites. Two hymns score nine requests, H. F. Lyte's *Praise my soul the king of heaven*, and Cecil Frances Alexander's *There is a green hill*. Among the sevens are *Love divine all loves excelling*, *Praise to the holiest* and *The Lord's my shepherd*, and the sixes are *Breathe on me breath of God*, *Come down O Love divine*, *Dear Lord and Father of*

*Mankind, Guide me O Thou Great Jehovah, Jesus Lover of my
soul, Praise to the Lord the Almighty,* and *Thy hand O God
has guided.*

The British "forty-eight", as one would expect, are
all known and used in Australia, thirty of them "frequently" and eighteen "very infrequently" though this
latter list most surprisingly includes *All people that on
earth do dwell, O God of Bethel,* and *Soldiers of Christ Arise.*
Australia too—through the supervision of religious
broadcasts of the A.B.C.—puts forward its own eleven
(given alphabetically):

TATE AND BRADY	As pants the hart
THRING	Fierce raged the tempest
FABER	Hark, hark, my soul
NEWTON	How sweet the Name of Jesus
ST. BERNARD	Jesus Thou joy of loving hearts
EDMESTON	Lead us Heavenly Father
HOLMES	Lord of all being
RINKART	Now thank we all our God
WESLEY	O Thou who camest
BUDRY	Thine is the glory
BULLOCK AND BAKER	We love the place O God

An excellent supporting eleven: not exactly a winning
team amongst the giants but containing some fine exhibition players!

The Canadian Broadcasting Corporation has checked
through its hymn files in Toronto, and amongst the
records of hymns used for community singing and
services are all the British "forty-eight" plus another
thirty favourites amongst Canada's hymn-lovers. I note
some of these as unexpected absentees in the British list,

STONE	The Church's one foundation
COWPER	God moves in a mysterious way

MONSELL	Fight the good fight
WESLEY	O for a thousand tongues
WATTS	When I survey the wondrous cross
ALEXANDER	All things bright and beautiful
DODDRIDGE	Awake my soul stretch every nerve
GLADDEN	O Master let me walk with Thee
MATHESON	O Love that wilt not let me go
FABER	Hark, hark, my soul
AUBER	Our blest Redeemer ere He breathed

This makes another eleven of the first quality which would find their supporters everywhere.

In comparing the British forty-eight with the Australian and Canadian lists it appears that Britain too has an eleven, a kind of distinguished "tail-end" which neither Australia nor Canada brings on to the field:

DA SIENA	Come down O Love divine
AINGER	God is working His purpose out
GELLERT	Jesus lives! thy terrors now
ELLIOTT	Thou didst leave thy throne
PLUMPTRE	Thy hand O God has guided
KELLY	The head that once was crowned with thorns
	We sing the praise of Him who died
KETHE	All people that on earth do dwell
BUNYAN	He who would valiant be
HERBERT	Let all the world in every corner sing
ELLERTON	Saviour again to thy dear name

Each of these hymns scores at least four in the B.B.C.'s innings, and two of them six. Looking at Britain, Australia and Canada together it seems that out of the immense range of hymns available the three countries put twenty hymns ahead of all the rest, at least those are the ones which, according to radio choices, they most frequently ask to sing.

I give the list in alphabetical order:

LYTE	Abide with me
PERRONET	All hail the power of Jesu's name
HATCH	Breathe on me, Breath of God
BRIDGES	Crown Him with many crowns
WHITTIER	Dear Lord and Father of Mankind
HOW	For all the saints
NEWTON	Glorious things of thee are spoken
WILLIAMS	Guide me O Thou great Jehovah
ALEXANDER	Jesus calls us
WESLEY	Jesus Lover of my soul
WATTS	Jesus shall reign
NEWMAN	Lead kindly light
GERHARDT	O sacred head sore wounded
LYTE	Praise my soul
NEWMAN	Praise to the Holiest
WESLEY	Rejoice, the Lord is King
MERRILL	Rise up O men of God
ELLERTON	The day thou gavest
PSALM 23	The Lord's my shepherd
ALEXANDER	There is a green hill

But for Australia's "fine" placing of six famous hymns as amongst those "sung very infrequently" the list would also have included:

MILTON	Let us with a gladsome mind
DODDRIDGE	O God of Bethel
WESLEY	Soldiers of Christ arise
CLEPHANE	Beneath the Cross of Jesus
HEBER	Holy, holy, holy
BARING-GOULD	Now the day is over

II

The twenty "winners" of the Commonwealth now face the mighty wave of hymn-singing which since 1800 has swept across the United States of America. Religious life in the United States with its "camp meeting" traditions, its "conventions", its regional divisions and the mixing of so many varied national strains in the melting pot was bound to produce its own hymns. The "folk songs" of the southern States too were religious, the negro spirituals,

> Go down Moses, way down in Egypt land,
> Tell ole Pharaoh, let my people go—

and the host of poignant and moving companion spirituals built themselves into the hymn memory of a people in the making.

Then came the "gospel song" period, gathered round the revivals of Moody and Sankey in the 1870's, with its author-phenomenon the blind Fanny Crosby who between eight and eighty years of age wrote at least eight thousand song-hymns, many of which went round the world and are still sung, such as *Safe in the arms of Jesus, Rescue the perishing, Blessed assurance Jesus is mine*. Fanny Crosby may not have been a hymn-writer of the first order, but her "spiritual ditties" affected popular religion in the English speaking world, and still help to decide what hymns America likes to sing, in addition to the great classics which are shared by other hymn-lovers.

Arthur Austin, author of *Favorite Hymns of the United States*, groups ten hymns, which he says are the "top ten" with little doubt, in the United States in the following order of preference (*see also list on* p. 68):

WESLEY	Jesus Lover of My Soul
BENNARD	The Old Rugged Cross
MILES	In the Garden
HAWKS	I need Thee every hour
TOPLADY	Rock of Ages

LYTE	Abide with me
BARING-GOULD	Now the day is over
SCRIVEN	What a Friend we have in Jesus
ADAMS	Nearer my God to Thee
NEWMAN	Lead kindly Light

The second and third hymns, while known elsewhere, would rarely come into a list of non-American first choices. It is also surprising to see *Abide with me* in the sixth place behind *Rock of Ages*, which, in spite of its fame and romantic traditions, is not chosen in Britain so often as is supposed. The American "gospel melody" tradition is also seen in *I need Thee every hour* and in *What a Friend we have in Jesus* both of which, however, have had a welcome across the Atlantic.

The "top ten" in the United States are, according to Arthur Austin, accompanied by another nine which cannot be placed in any order of preference. They could be moved up and down without offending anyone's hymn susceptibilities. I give them in alphabetical order:

FAWCETT	Blest be the tie that binds
FABER	Faith of our fathers
RANKIN	God be with you till we meet again
HEBER	Holy, holy, holy
BENNETT	In the sweet by and by
BARING-GOULD	Onward! Christian Soldiers
WATTS	Our God our help in ages past
THOMPSON	Softly and tenderly Jesus is calling
WALFORD	Sweet hour of prayer

This group might be called "the hymns of friendship and sentiment", a happy combination of tender human memories and simple faith a little too cloying for some, but nevertheless a popular mixture whenever it is taken. The surprise is to see Watts' *Our God our help* in this list rather than amongst the "top ten", but this international anthem does not seem to be demanded except on those national occasions when it takes its place by right and almost without invitation. Like the universal Christmas and Easter hymns and carols, which have been excluded from comment in this book, Watts' hymn has its own unshakeable place.

So with the United States' choice in the arena it is possible to assemble the favourite hymns of the English speaking world. They number just a hundred, a surprisingly small group out of so vast a field, and it is that hundred that have been written about.

III

But it is tempting to carry the poll for the most popular even further. What hymns are chosen against all comers? What hymns appear in any list of hymns in whatever country where hymns are sung in English? In a word, is there a topmost, all-conquering hymn?

The choice clearly lies between Charles Wesley's *Jesus Lover of My Soul* and Henry Lyte's *Abide with me*, and I think there is no doubt that with America overwhelmingly in favour of *Jesus Lover*, and the one additional "request" it gets in B.B.C. choices, Charles Wesley's hymn is the winner. Third place goes to Henry Newman's *Lead kindly Light*, which is the only other hymn which appears in all lists. Two other hymns almost tie with Newman's hymn, Heber's *Holy, holy, holy*, and Baring-Gould's *Now the day is over*, but as Australia did not put them in its first flight of thirty, they fell back a point.

So with a hundred hymns out of the many thousands

in English the next stage is to arrange them in a sequence as a good hymn-book would do.

They fall most naturally into five categories: Hymns of Praise, Hymns of Prayer, Hymns of Experience, Hymns of Christ and His Church, and Hymns of Christian Action. Any other hymn-lover would undoubtedly arrange them differently, and readers may care to do so, and let me know how their lists work out.

A hymn, like a good book, is a very personal creation, and a hymn with many years of history behind it is inter-twined with all sorts of personal and sacred experiences. These are the ones which hymn-singers in the English speaking world have made their own, and which they choose to sing under all sorts of circumstances.

It is a melancholy thought that of the seventy-eight authors, who are listed with their dates on pp. 167-8, only eighteen lived in the twentieth century. From this it would seem that the golden age of hymn-writing was in the late eighteenth and early nineteenth centuries. Fifty-three of the authors were clergy and ministers, and eleven were women. Hymn-writing seems to attract both the lowly and the exalted. In the list are Bunyan, Cowper, Milton, Kipling, Newman and Whittier, but in the ranks are the many men and women whose one hymn has given them a niche amongst the immortals.

HYMNS OF PRAISE

ST. FRANCIS	*All creatures of our God and King*
WILLIAM KETHE	*All people that on earth do dwell*
C. F. ALEXANDER	*All things bright and beautiful*
ISAAC WATTS	*Before Jehovah's aweful throne*
W. W. HOW	*For all the saints*
REGINALD HEBER	*Holy, holy, holy, Lord God Almighty*
W. C. SMITH	*Immortal, invisible*
GEORGE HERBERT	*Let all the world in every corner sing*
JOHN MILTON	*Let us with a gladsome mind*
O. W. HOLMES	*Lord of all being*
M. RINKART	*Now thank we all our God*
H. F. LYTE	*Praise, my soul, the King of heaven*
J. H. NEWMAN	*Praise to the holiest*
J. NEANDER	*Praise to the Lord, the Almighty*
CHARLES WESLEY	*Rejoice, the Lord is King*
E. BUDRY	*Thine is the glory*
PSALM 121	*Unto the hills*

1

HYMNS OF PRAISE

THE seventeen hymns whose stories are told in this section cover the whole range of "Praise to God" which, after all is said and done about hymns, is the chief purpose of hymn-singing.

The greatest of the praise hymns find their inspiration in the Psalms, and indeed are but more singable ways of using the Psalms.

Some hymns in the other sections might well have come into this section. For instance, *O God of Bethel* was moved from this section to "Hymns of Experience". Where do Praise and Experience separate? It is arguable that *For all the saints* is out of place here, but it is surely a mighty anthem of praise as well as much else.

There is a lot of Christian doctrine too in this section —God as the God of creation, God's Providence and Care, and His Eternal Fatherhood, and then God as a Loving and Redemptive God as in *Praise to the holiest*.

One is glad to note that Australia is singing *Thine is the glory*, which is happily winning its way as the ecumenical praise hymn. To hear a great international gathering of Christians singing it—each in his tongue— is a moving experience. What a pity the hymn is missing from many modern hymn-books.

ALL CREATURES OF OUR GOD AND KING

Francis of Assisi

OUTSIDE the little town of Assisi in Italy you come to the group of buildings called St. Damian. There on a summer day in July 1225 came St. Francis, ill, blind and lonely, knowing that he would get comfort from the Poor Clares and especially his friend St. Clara.

The quiet courtyard of St. Damian, still much the same to-day, was a haven of rest, and there Francis in his brown habit and sandalled feet, tired and depressed, sat down. Clara's women busied themselves to look after the man to whom they all owed so much, and down in the garden they quickly put up a little cell of reeds so that he could be by himself undisturbed.

An army of rats and mice also lived in the garden and ran over his bed at night. But sleeping on the ground in those conditions was nothing unusual for Francis, and he came up to the house for his meals with his old gaiety returning. "A single sunbeam", he used to say, "is enough to drive away many shadows." The sisters began to hear songs and laughter coming from the hut as if Francis was composing something new.

One day at the table of the Poor Clares, between July and September 1225, Francis spoke his *Canticle of the Sun*,

> Praised be my Lord God with all his creatures and especially our brother the sun. . . .

This Beatitude of Praise for all the wonder of God's creation stands amongst the great praise hymns of the world, and W. H. Draper's rendering of it is the one used in most hymn-books.

In it St. Francis seems to capture much of his teaching and example about loving the simple things of life and

26

aising God for them. It was almost the last great act
his life, for in a year (October 1226) he welcomed
sister death" while the birds flocked round and sang
songs "even gladder than their wont".

> All creatures of our God and King,
> Lift up your voice and with us sing
> Alleluia, alleluia!
> Thou burning sun with golden beam,
> Thou silver moon with softer gleam:
>
> Thou rushing wind that art so strong,
> Ye clouds that sail in heaven along,
> O praise Him, alleluia!
> Thou rising morn, in praise rejoice,
> Ye lights of evening, find a voice:

This rendering by W. H. Draper came out of one of
the great singing counties of England—Yorkshire—and
was done for a schoolchildren's festival in the city of
Leeds.

ALL PEOPLE THAT ON EARTH DO DWELL

William Kethe

WHAT a magnificent start William Kethe's version of Psalm 100 makes to a hymn-book. His four stately verses set to the *Old Hundredth* have graced many notable occasions, and form one of the most successful of the adaptations of the Psalms.

Although he was a Scot, William Kethe may have written his hymn in the green and pleasant vale of Blackmoor in Dorset, deep in the heart of rural England, for in the years between 1560 and 1570 he was nominally Rector of Childe Okeford near Blandford. There is no memorial of him in the old church with its eye on the Dorset downs, but his hymn is worth a good many brass tablets.

Before he had this Dorset living he was mixed up in the "Reformation troubles" on the Continent and was a kind of messenger between England and the exiles in Basel and Strasbourg. Many of his Psalm versions were published in Geneva (perhaps this one was), and reached Scotland, too. But *All People* is the most renowned of his versions and it is easy to see why.

If you read Psalm 100 alongside the hymn, you will see that Kethe takes the salient points of the Psalm, and, without fuss or decoration, puts them into verse. The Psalm in the Authorized Version takes five verses; Kethe does it in four—four of the greatest verses of praise in the English language.

ALL THINGS BRIGHT AND BEAUTIFUL

Cecil Frances Alexander

THIS hymn—amongst the "number one" hymns for children—came out of the green heart of Ireland, for its author Mrs. Alexander lived all her life there:

> The purple-headed mountain,
> The river running by,
> The sunset, and the morning
> That brightens up the sky.

That might be a description of the mixture of mountain, river and sky which Mrs. Alexander saw every day of her life in counties Tyrone and Londonderry. Her husband, Dr. Alexander, was Bishop of Derry, and she began writing poems for children because of a complaint by her godsons. They found that learning the Church Catechism was a dull business. So their godmother tried her hand at writing little verses to help the boys along with their catechism.

The first belief of the catechism is, "I believe in God the Father, who hath made me, and all the world," and when you are singing *All things bright and beautiful* the very serious purpose of the author comes out in the famous refrain,

> The Lord God made them all

and in the last verse, too,

> How great is God Almighty,
> Who has made all things well.

Mrs. Alexander's hymn is often thought of as one of the happy hymns celebrating the natural scene, but like all her four hundred hymns it has a teaching purpose within its very happy, easy flowing verses.

BEFORE JEHOVAH'S AWEFUL THRONE

Isaac Watts

As a young man Isaac Watts lived in Southampton where he was born in 1674, from where nowadays the great ships set sail across the Atlantic. The lovely view across Southampton Water is said to have inspired his hymn *There is a land of pure delight*. It is more than likely that the bad hymns—as he thought them—in the Southampton chapel he worshipped in stirred him to write some better ones. Hymn-writing was a bold venture for a young man, but Isaac Watts (*see also p.* 99) was the grandson of a bold Cromwellian naval officer who served under the redoubtable Admiral Blake, and he himself at twenty-eight was pastor of the famous Mark Lane Chapel in London.

His pen won even a mightier battle than his grandfather's sword. Isaac Watts laid the foundations of all English hymn-singing, and made a place for the hymn in public worship. He was masterful enough to straighten out the metrical psalms, which dominated public worship, and gave a chance to the people to sing.

For instance he found the Scottish version of Psalm 20—for most of his great hymns are linked with the Psalms—in this condition,

> In chariots some put confidence
> Some horses trust upon;
> But we remember will the name
> Of our Lord God alone

and left it in this more melodious state:

> Some trust in horses train'd for war
> And some of chariots make their boasts;
> Our surest expectations are
> From Thee, the Lord of heav'nly hosts.

30

You see him at work too in this hymn *Before Jehovah's Aweful Throne* which is more spacious than William Kethe on the same theme. The last verse in particular is thoroughly Wattsian:

> Wide as the world is Thy command;
>   Vast as eternity Thy love;
> Firm as a rock Thy truth must stand,
>   When rolling years shall cease to move.

The last line is a powerful one. It makes the Christian faith part of the universe, and yet dares to believe that beyond the span of time God's truth stands firm. It is a theme that Isaac Watts takes up in others of his great hymns which are mentioned elsewhere.

> Before Jehovah's aweful throne,
>   Ye nations, bow with sacred joy;
> Know that the Lord is God alone;
>   He can create and He destroy.

Watts' verse is a potent reminder in the atomic age that the last dread secrets of the universe are with God and not with man. No hymn more majestically sets man in relation to his Creator, and at the same time lifts man to his rightful place—without pride or pomp— in the ordered universe.

FOR ALL THE SAINTS

William Walsham How

THIS great hymn of Bishop How's is placed amongst the Praise hymns, but no doubt it rightly belongs as well to the hymns of the Church, and perhaps even more appropriately to the Thanksgiving hymns. Its modern use in memorial services has helped to keep its purpose clear as a hymn of the Church Triumphant, and no hymn rides more spaciously away from earthly to heavenly things, or so realistically bears the singer with it.

Like Bishop Heber (*see* p. 33) William Walsham How lived in Shropshire, indeed he was born in Shrewsbury and went to its famous school. He was always busy with his pen, and there are said to be three score of his hymns in various books. In 1888 he became first Bishop of Wakefield, and died in 1897.

For twenty-six years Walsham How was a country parson in a remote bit of country on the borders of England and Wales, at Whittington near Oswestry, travelling the country roads to his canon's duties at St. Asaph's Cathedral, the smallest of cathedrals but one well provided with its own saints. In front of the cathedral is a memorial to those bishops who in 1588 first translated the Bible into Welsh, and within are a tablet and window to the memory of Mrs. Hemans, the poet and hymn-writer, author of *Answer me, burning stars of light*, who lived in St. Asaph's.

HOLY, HOLY, HOLY, LORD GOD ALMIGHTY

Reginald Heber

How many great hymns have come out of the quiet places in the English countryside? Reginald Heber's hymn, nearly always associated with morning worship, is one of them, for he wrote it during his sixteen years' ministry at Hodnet in Shropshire between 1807 and 1823, but not as a morning hymn.

If you turn to the fourth chapter of Revelation, and to verses 8–11, there is Heber's hymn. The rhythm, too, of his hymn is there, but how much more singable are his verses. It is a hymn to the Trinity.

In his quiet country vicarage Reginald Heber used to dream dreams of far places. He would take out a map of India and trace imaginary journeys on it, and when his dreams came true in 1823—on being made Bishop of Calcutta—he left behind his hymn-writing days for the missionary adventure itself. But not before he had written the most famous of all missionary hymns, *From Greenland's icy mountains*, and a greatly loved children's hymn, *By cool Siloam's shady rill (see p. 62)*.

On the Saturday evening before Whit Sunday in 1819 Heber was asked by his father-in-law, the Dean of St. Asaph's, who was to preach next day at Wrexham, for "something for them to sing in the morning". Heber moved away to another part of the room and quickly wrote out the four verses of the hymn, which was sung on the Sunday for the first time.

Heber travelled far and wide in India during his brief three years as bishop before he suddenly died in 1826. The three hymns mentioned and his Christmas hymn *Brightest and Best of the Sons of the Morning* are sure of being sung as long as hymns are sung. But *Holy, holy, holy*, evidently stands first amongst the choices.

IMMORTAL, INVISIBLE, GOD ONLY WISE

Walter Chalmers Smith

It is said of the French painter Gauguin that he died broken-hearted because he was never able to "paint light", that elusive wonder of creation artists see but never fully grasp. One is reminded of this when singing this hymn in which Walter Chalmers Smith links God with "light",

> Unresting, unhasting, and silent as light.

He puts, in one line, all that baffled Gauguin,

> In light inaccessible hid from our eyes.

Walter Chalmers Smith was an Aberdonian, and it may be that his sense of light came from his youthful days in that handsome Scottish city where the sun on the granite buildings makes them glisten like silver. Or was it the undying light of day which never really fades out in the summer nights of those latitudes?

As a minister in London and Edinburgh Chalmers Smith wrote a great deal of poetry, but this one hymn which is on the "choices" list of Britain and Australia gives him an honoured place amongst hymn-writers. He was Moderator of the Free Church of Scotland in 1893. He died at the age of 84 in 1908.

LET ALL THE WORLD IN EVERY CORNER SING

George Herbert

TWENTY miles across the Dorset and Wiltshire downs from the Childe Okeford of William Kethe (*see* p. 28) lies another rural gem of England, "sweet Bemerton" on the little river Nadder just outside the city of Salisbury.

There between 1630 and 1632 George Herbert, author of this hymn, was rector. He could see two wonderful sights from his rectory windows still to be seen; the spire of Salisbury Cathedral and a gracious glimpse of Wilton, one of the loveliest private houses in England.

Although he died when he was only forty George Herbert has left his mark on the Church of England as the model of a country parson. His family at Bemerton was a school of religion, for he used to say, "in the house of a preacher all are preachers". His parish was a well-visited one, Herbert going on horseback over the high and windy uplands round Bemerton. He was parish doctor, lawyer and peacemaker, and his house was always open to parishioners however humble they were. When at evening time the candles were brought into the rooms of the rectory the household repeated, "God send us the light of heaven".

Herbert was plain Christian goodness even though he had a touch of fear and terror in his teaching, as in the verse he used to teach to the children in the parish,

> Fear God, my child, be brave and wise,
> And speak the truth, and tell no lies;
> For liars shall for ever dwell
> With devils in the hottest hell.

John and Charles Wesley thought so much of Herbert's

verses that they introduced forty of them into their *Hymns and Sacred Poems*, but the one hymn the world remembers Herbert by is *Let all the world* with its atmosphere of light, sun and air which he knew in his country parish. Perhaps the order and reverence of his country household are reflected in *Teach me my God and King*, the other hymn we owe this saintly countryman.

The busy rush of modern traffic sweeps past Bemerton nowadays, but the village holds its own secret in its still peaceful meadows,

> Let all the world in every corner sing
>   My God and King!
> The Church with psalms must shout,
> No door can keep them out:
> But above all, the heart
> Must bear the longest part.
> Let all the world in every corner sing
>   My God and King!

LET US WITH A GLADSOME MIND

John Milton

IT is a pleasant bit of exercise for the hymn-lover to take a copy of Milton's Poems, his Bible—open at Psalm 136—and a modern collection of hymns with *Let us with a gladsome mind* in it and see what happens in the process of making a psalm-hymn fit for modern singers to sing.

There are twenty-four stanzas in Milton's paraphrase of the Psalm, but most hymn-books usually give a short selection, and two of them are usually starred in case the congregation gets exhausted with the refrain,

> For His mercies ay endure
> Ever faithful, ever sure.

But the original has some stalwart verses about the crossing of the Red Sea,

> The floods stood still like walls of glass,
> While the Hebrew bands did pass.

> But full soon they did devour
> The Tawny King with all his power.

And then when the crossing was safely done,

> And large-lim'd *Og* he did subdue,
> With all his over hardy crew.

Milton stuck very closely to the Scripture version of the Psalm, and in his day they liked their facts tough and untrimmed. This fine old hymn-psalm stands high amongst the choices of British radio listeners. It is a favourite for community hymn singing, and it may be used most effectively as "grace before meat" on festive occasions.

37

With all the majesty of his immortal poetry, and his place amongst the prophets of liberty, it is pleasant to see Milton in the hymn-books and hear him sung with gusto.

There are some memorable lines which although sung often and loud are never dimmed,

> Let us *blaze* His name abroad
> For of gods He is the God:

This is a piece of sound missionary theology which acknowledges no truck with other gods or religions. It comes out of the authentic fastness of the Old Testament where, however, the jealousy of the one true God is always married with his tender love and care,

> He hath with a *piteous* eye,
> Looked upon our misery:

Piteous means loving, and *misery* stands for our general condition. Milton may need some interpretation for the present world of English speaking people but his last verse needs no commentary,

> Let us therefore warble forth
> His high majesty and worth:
> *For His mercies ay endure,*
> *Ever faithful, ever sure.*

LORD OF ALL BEING, THRONED AFAR

Oliver Wendell Holmes

HARVARD in the United States, like the Cambridge of England from which John Harvard came, has been a home of scholarly poets. One of them, Oliver Wendell Holmes, although a professor of anatomy and distinguished in his own professional world, gained wider fame as a writer.

But for one person who nowadays reads his *Autocrat at the Breakfast Table* and his *Professor at the Breakfast Table* a thousand sing his hymn,

> Lord of all being, throned afar,
> Thy glory flames from sun and star;
> Centre and soul of every sphere,
> Yet to each loving heart how near.

He threw off the beliefs of his orthodox Christian upbringing and became a Unitarian, but his hymn, like all sincere hymn-writing, has won its way and is sung now by all denominations.

In his witty, punning style Wendell Holmes called it "A Sun-Day hymn" when it appeared in the *Atlantic Monthly* for December 1859.

His other hymn deserves to be better known,

> Our Father! while our hearts unlearn
>   The creeds that wrong Thy name,
> Still let our hallowed altars burn
>   With Faith's undying flame.

The first two lines may reflect his own change of theological position, but it is more likely that Holmes was rebelling against evil in general, for his last verse runs,

39

Our prayers accept; our sins forgive;
   Our youthful zeal renew;
Shape for us holier lives to live,
   And nobler work to do.

Holmes had the reasonable, cultured man's religion.
His hymns add dignity to any hymn-book.

But this one of popular choice has a warmth and
personality which are perhaps lacking in the others,

Lord of all life, below, above,
Whose light is truth, whose warmth is love,
Before Thy ever-blazing throne
We ask no lustre of our own.

Grant us Thy truth to make us free,
And kindling hearts that burn for Thee,
Till all Thy living altars claim
One holy light, one heavenly flame.

NOW THANK WE ALL OUR GOD

Martin Rinkart

THE little town of Eilenburg in Saxony in Germany had walls round it in the seventeenth century, and when the troubles of the Thirty Years' War fell on the country-side refugees flocked into it for safety. Plague and famine followed them. People died at the rate of fifty a day, and the sad and heavy task of Christian burial fell mainly on one minister, Martin Rinkart. In all over eight thousand people died, and amongst them was Rinkart's own wife.

But in the midst of all his harrowing sorrow Rinkart went on with his music and his poetry. He had sung as a boy in the famous choir of St. Thomas's Leipzig, and his delight in the songs and folk melodies of his country-men were there to cheer him. He even wrote dramas to be acted in public, and his native Eilenburg puts him first amongst her sons, although like many men he had little honour at home in his own day.

The two verses of his hymn are based on Ecclus. 50: 22-24:

> Now therefore bless ye the God of all, which only doeth wondrous things every where, which exalteth our days from the womb, and dealeth with us according to his mercy.
>
> He grant us joyfulness of heart, and that peace may be in our days in Israel for ever:
>
> That he would confirm his mercy with us, and deliver us at his time!

PRAISE, MY SOUL, THE KING OF HEAVEN

Henry Francis Lyte

BASED on the 103rd Psalm, Henry Lyte's stately hymn of praise has probably begun more solemn ceremonies than any hymn in the English language. Lyte himself is of course more immediately connected with his hymn *Abide with me* (*see* p. 54), but the story of his hymn-writing goes back to the time when he was a curate at Marazion in Cornwall where he had come after his college days in Dublin. There, when he was twenty-five, he had a deep religious experience caused by the illness and death of a brother clergyman.

This experience turned Lyte from being a conventional and formal clergyman, with a gift for versifying, into a poet with a religious message. He says that the death of his friend "who died happy in the thought that there was *One* who would atone for his delinquencies" made him "study my Bible and preach in another manner than I had previously done".

This free paraphrase of Psalm 103 was published in his book *Spirit of the Psalms* in 1834 when he was in his ministry at Brixham, the Devon fishing port. The Brixham fishermen are famous for their gallantry and daring in the stormy waters of the Atlantic fishing grounds, and Lyte's hymn has something of the tenderness of strong men in dangerous places:

> Father-like He tends and spares us;
>   Well our feeble frame He knows;
> In His hands He gently bears us,
>   Rescues us from all our foes:

Modern singing practice however gives women's and children's voices only the privilege of singing it! The hymn was chosen by Queen Elizabeth for her wedding to the Duke of Edinburgh on November 20, 1947— also the day of the centenary of Lyte's death.

Lyte captures the measure of the Psalm in unforgettable verses. It has time, eternity, God and man all locked in its embrace, and its last verse has the soaring quality of high religion. In one grand sweep the writer brings the whole created universe into the act of praise,

> Angels, help us to adore Him,
>   Ye behold Him face to face;
> Sun and moon, bow down before Him,
>   Dwellers all in time and space:
>   Praise Him! praise Him!
>   Praise with us the God of grace!

PRAISE TO THE HOLIEST IN THE HEIGHT

John Henry Newman

In the dark winter days of 1865 a man might have been seen piecing together odd scraps of paper in his little room at the Oratory, Birmingham. Those scraps of paper are still kept there as a precious remembrance of J. H. Newman and the poem he wrote in such a strange manner. It was *The Dream of Gerontius*. Newman wrote, "It came into my head to write it, I really can't tell how. And I wrote on till it was finished."

Like all Newman wrote, there is a lot of himself in *The Dream of Gerontius*, the story of the pilgrimage of a soul through the experience of death to the light of the presence of Christ.

Set to Elgar's music *The Dream of Gerontius* has gone round the world; but the bit that most people know and recognize is the twenty-eight lines beginning *Praise to the Holiest in the Height*—Newman's celebration of the great act of redemption,

> Simply to His grace and wholly
> Light and life and strength belong,
> And I love, supremely, solely,
> Him the holy, Him the strong.

Many feel that this great hymn lacks a finish. After

> . . . the garden secretly,
> And on the Cross on high,

Newman might have added another verse celebrating the Resurrection and the Ascension to complete the hymn. But Newman's own pilgrimage was strife rather than triumph—"in the garden" at night rather than in the Resurrection light. The hymn is about Newman himself and his religious life, and when we sing it we touch saint as well as hymn-writer.

PRAISE TO THE LORD, THE ALMIGHTY

Joachim Neander

How many famous hymns were written for the eye of the writer only? This is one of them. Joachim Neander was only a young man of thirty when he died in his home town of Bremen, Germany, in 1680, so his hymns have a young man's experiences in them.

This one probably grew out of a difficult experience when he was a schoolmaster at Düsseldorf in the Rhineland. He could not get on with the minister and elders of the Reformed Church who controlled the school. They criticized him for starting separate prayer meetings and for not coming to the parish Holy Communion. No doubt Joachim was "uppish" and believed that his personal religious experience was superior to anybody else's. There was an enquiry and Joachim was suspended from his post for fourteen days and then reinstated as schoolmaster.

He was probably a moody young man who liked lonely walks, particularly up the lovely Neanderthal down which flows the little river Düssel. There he found a cave to retreat to and to note down his poems, which were widely circulated after his death. German hymnbooks included them, and through the skilful adaptations of Catherine Winckworth who collected his hymns in her *Lyra Germanica* (1855) this spacious hymn is a memorial to his sensitive spirit.

REJOICE, THE LORD IS KING

Charles Wesley

OUT of the thousands of hymns which Charles Wesley (*see* p. 128) wrote six appear among the predominant choices of the English speaking peoples. They are,

> Jesus Lover of my soul
> Rejoice, the Lord is King
> Love divine all loves excelling
> O for a thousand tongues to sing
> O thou who camest from above
> Ye servants of God

To have written these six alone—or any one of them —would be a proud accomplishment for any hymn-writer. But the eighteenth child of Samuel and Susanna Wesley kept going at high-level hymn-writing all his life.

There is no explaining a genius, but there are some reasons for Charles's success. He wrote for a particular people, "called Methodists", and made hymns and hymn-singing an equivalent for them of the Psalms, the Prayer Book and the Canon of the Mass. He stuck closely also to the great events of the Christian faith. He was never far away from what God does for man, and man's response to the Divine Love. His hymns are Scriptural hymns—only five books of the Bible are not illustrated in the hymns. Charles Wesley had a knack, a facility perhaps, for hymn-writing, but it was a well disciplined one; the swing and measure of his hymns never desert them.

The six hymns—a little hymn-book in themselves— start off with *Rejoice, the Lord is King*, a joyful gallop which like many of Wesley's hymns begins as power-fully as it ends,

> Mortals give thanks and sing
> And triumph evermore

which is matched with

> We soon shall hear the archangel's voice,
> The trump of God shall sound rejoice!

There are hymns of Wesley more loved than this one, and some which speak to the heart more tenderly, but for hymn-writing in its evangelical prime, with one idea to each line, and no awkward ends, *Rejoice the Lord* stands supreme,

> Lift up your heart, lift up your voice:
> Rejoice, again I say, rejoice!

No one but a master could match such mounting simplicity and repetition at the same time. And no one who was not grounded in a theology of experience would have dared, in five short verses, to compass the whole range of revealed religion. This is a hymn of the Kingdom in its divine consummation, a triumphant celebration of "who Jesus is"—not a teacher, not a prophet, not a seer, not a leader, but the King,

> His kingdom cannot fail;
>   He rules o'er earth and heaven;
> The keys of death and hell
>   Are to our Jesus given.

THINE IS THE GLORY

Edmond Budry
trs. Richard Birch Hoyle

IT was Sunday, August 22, 1948, in the city of Amsterdam. The square outside the great Nieuwe Kerk was alive with people gathering for the opening service of the first Assembly of the World Council of Churches. They had come from scores of countries and a hundred and fifty churches to begin the great encounter of "staying together" in the name of Christ.

One caught glimpses of archbishops and Congregationalists, patriarchs and Methodists, archimandrites and Baptists, little men from the Karen hills of Burma, fair-haired men from Scandinavia, broad-faced ones from China, delegates from India, Africa and Japan, and the more familiar figures from the English speaking lands.

Inside the church a procession was formed which sang *All people that on earth do dwell* from the hymn-book "Cantate Domino" which gives over a hundred great hymns in many languages. After prayers, and the Scriptures in French and Swedish, we stood to sing *Thine is the glory*, to a stately melody from Handel's "Judas Maccabeus", written in French by Edmond Budry in 1884,

> *A toi la gloire O Ressuscité*
> *A toi la victoire pour l'éternité.*
> *Brillant de lumière, l'ange est descendu,*
> *Il roule la pierre du tombeau vaincu.*

which Richard Birch Hoyle translates

> Thine is the glory, Risen conqu'ring Son,
> Endless is the vict'ry Thou o'er death hast won.
> Angels in bright raiment rolled the stone away,
> Kept the folded grave-clothes, where Thy body lay.

48

With the first two lines as a refrain the fine hymn filled the great church with a noble volume of glorious praise, and has become the universal anthem of the ecumenical movement. Edmond Budry was pastor for thirty-five years at Vevey on Lake Geneva, and wrote over sixty hymns many of which appeared in the hymn-book *Chants Evangeliques*.

The translator of this hymn, R. B. Hoyle (1875–1939), was an English Baptist minister with remarkable linguistic gifts. For "Cantate Domino" he did translations from twelve languages. His free translations always manage to capture the spirit of the original, as in verse two of this hymn,

> *Vois-le paraître: C'est lui, c'est Jésus,*
> *Ton Sauveur, ton Maître! Oh! ne doute plus;*
> *Sois dans l'allégresse——Peuple du Seigneur,*
> *Et redis sans cesse—Que Christ est vainqueur!*

> Lo Jesus meets thee—Risen from the tomb;
> Lovingly He greets thee—Scatters fear and gloom;
> Let His church with gladness—Hymns of triumph sing,
> For her Lord now liveth; Death hath lost its sting.

UNTO THE HILLS

John Campbell, ninth Duke of Argyll

THIS is Canada's own free rendering of the 121st Psalm,

Unto the hills around do I lift up my longing eyes

which was a present to the Canadian people from the Governor—the Duke of Argyll, who as Marquis of Lorne was Governor-General of Canada from 1878 to 1883. Just before he took up his duties in Canada he issued a collection of paraphrases of the Psalms, and this one immediately appealed to the Canadian people. It has not, perhaps, the direct and rugged simplicity of the Scottish paraphrase, "I to the hills will lift mine eyes", but Canada loves it and sings it by choice.

2

HYMNS OF PRAYER

HYMNS OF PRAYER

H. F. LYTE	*Abide with me*
TATE AND BRADY	*As pants the hart*
H. TWELLS	*At even when the sun was set*
HELEN TAYLOR	*Bless this house*
EDWIN HATCH	*Breathe on me, Breath of God*
R. HEBER	*By cool Siloam's shady rill*
J. G. WHITTIER	*Dear Lord and Father of mankind*
J. E. RANKIN	*God be with you till we meet again*
A. L. WARING	*In heavenly love abiding*
W. W. WALFORD	*Sweet hour of prayer*

ABIDE WITH ME

Henry Francis Lyte

ONE of the great national sporting events in Britain each year is the Cup Tie at Wembley when the two conquering football teams which have fought their way through the cup games of the year meet for decisive battle. The huge Wembley stadium seats over a hundred thousand people, and while they are waiting for the match to begin the crowd sings. The management sets a programme of songs, and one year the popular song *Alexander's Rag-Time Band* was down to be sung. But the manager, Sir F. J. Wall, said afterwards,

> I felt impelled by a mysterious power. I was moved to run my pen through this item, and write beneath that *Abide with me* should be sung.

That started the annual custom which links Lyte's hymn with a great football occasion, and to hear a hundred thousand voices singing it in the open air is a tribute to the popular significance of the hymn.

Abide with me is often put amongst the evening hymns, but its place is not really there, nor did Lyte intend it to be, and the popular love of the hymn does not regard it so. It is really a contemplative prayer on the transitoriness of human life, the need of the soul for God, and the hope of a life to come. The hymn is almost too personal to be sung, but its very tenderness makes it speak for and to everyone.

It was Lyte's hymn which comforted and gave strength to Nurse Cavell when she faced the firing squad in Belgium in 1916, and it solaced Shackleton, too, in his companionship with death in the Antarctic snows, and it was played and sung as the doomed *Titanic* went down in the Atlantic in 1912 (*see* p. 90).

When the centenary of Lyte's death on November 20, 1847 was remembered in 1947 a flood of correspondence in the press bore witness to the hymn's power. One lady wrote to the London *Sunday Times*,

> Its secret is its great simplicity: it is easily grasped and understood by the ordinary man and its greatness, depth and beauty must appeal to scholars and thoughtful men whatever their religious conviction or creed.

A group of ex-prisoners of war wrote that every Sunday night in their Polish camp *Abide with me* was played—"furtive hands wiped away tears, and we were nearer home than at any other time". A famous regiment, The Royal Scots Fusiliers, still keeps up its custom of playing *Abide with me* on Sunday evenings too.

It is probable that Lyte shaped the hymn in his mind before he went to Brixham in Devon as rector when he was a young man of twenty-seven. It may have been the death of an old friend who constantly used the phrase "Abide with me" that fixed the three leading words of the hymn in his mind. No doubt his faithful pastorate of twenty-five years amongst the gallant fisherfolk of Brixham, regularly facing the perils of life and death, helped finally to shape the verses. Lyte's sensitive spirit must have been open to all the cares of his people always so near to the "eventide" of life themselves.

It was in the summer of 1847 after a last visit to Berry Head in Torbay that Lyte felt his own end was approaching, and just before he left to get the benefit of winter sunshine at Nice he handed the verses of *Abide with me* to his family. It was a legacy from which millions have benefited. Lyte lies in Nice cemetery.

The transatlantic cousin of his great hymn might be said to be Whittier's:

AS PANTS THE HART FOR COOLING STREAMS

Nahum Tate and Nicholas Brady

"TATE AND BRADY"—two names worth saluting in
the long story of how the Psalms were versified.

Both were Irishmen born within a few years of one
another, and they both flourished during the days of King
William III, and were strongly for the Protestant cause.

These two clergymen set out to give the Anglican
Church a new version of the versified Psalms. Everyone
in their day who cared for public worship was getting
tired of the version then in use, published over a
hundred years previously (1562) and edited by another
notable pair, "Sternhold and Hopkins":

> Sternhold and Hopkins had great qualms,
> When they translated David's psalms,
>   To make the heart right glad;
> But had it been King David's fate
> To hear thee sing and them translate,
>   By God 'twould set him mad.

So wrote the witty Lord Rochester to amuse Charles II
after morning worship when the clerk had been "whin-
ing, tooting, yelling, screeking". It was much the same
too in New England where the tyranny of *The Bay
Psalm Book* made a worshipper in Salem Church, Mass.,
scribble on a pew,

> Could poor King David but for once
> To Salem church repair,
> And hear his Psalms thus warbled out,
> Good Lord, how he would swear!

When Tate and Brady produced their New Version
in 1696 there were loud shouts from the opposition. But
there are some good things in it, and this versification
of Psalm 42 is one of the best.

AT EVEN WHEN THE SUN WAS SET

Henry Twells

No hymn in the English language breathes a more genuine piety and sense of prayer than this one. It is surprising that Canon Twells is not remembered by any other hymn that he wrote. But for this one we can be grateful. In the prime of his years (he was born in 1823) from 1856 to 1870 he was headmaster of a great London school, the Godolphin at Hammersmith, and was later an honorary canon of Peterborough Cathedral.

The first line of his hymn as printed above is now generally accepted instead of *At even ere the sun was set* although this line falls more gently on the ear. But *when* is certainly more Scripturally accurate than *ere* as both Mark 1: 32 and Luke 4: 40 prefer *when*. And Jewish custom supports it. No group of sick and diseased people would have gathered in the way that Canon Twells describes until the sun had set on the Sabbath day.

It is a pity that one of Canon Twells' verses is so often missed out in modern hymn collections:

> And some are pressed with worldly care,
>   And some are tried with sinful doubt;
> And some such grievous passions tear,
>   That only Thou canst cast them out.

A verse most apposite to modern life, and a prayer that most of us can make our own.

BLESS THIS HOUSE

Helen Taylor

WHEN does a sacred song become a hymn? It looks as if Helen Taylor's popular *Bless This House* has a foot in both camps. In Britain, where Helen Taylor wrote it in 1927, with musical setting by May Brahe, her song is famous as a solo:

> Bless this house, O Lord, we pray
> Make it safe by night and day:
> Bless these walls so firm and stout
> Keeping want and trouble out;
>
> Bless the roof and chimneys tall,
> Let Thy peace lie over all:
> Bless this door, that it may prove
> Ever open to joy and love.

In the United States it is frequently near the top in radio choices of popular hymns. During Thanksgiving Week especially—America's great home festival—it is one of the most played works.

John McCormack helped to make the song famous by his fine singing and recording of it. When McCormack appeared for the 25th season at the London Ballad Concerts in 1935 he asked Mr. Leslie Boosey to find him a suitable song to introduce. He was shown the song *Bless the House*, but with a singer's instinct for a word he suggested an alteration to *Bless This House*. So the title and the opening words were changed, and the song became immediately popular—particularly during the heavy bombing of British homes during the war.

Helen Taylor, the song writer, was the wife of Mr. Sydney H. Rothschild and was born in Britain in 1875 and died in 1943. Two other famous songs of hers are

I Passed By Your Window and *Come to The Fair*. Helen Taylor's simple lines of sincere homely sentiment make their instant appeal:

> Bless these windows shining bright,
> Letting in God's heavenly light:
> Bless the hearth ablazing there,
> With smoke ascending like a prayer:
>
> Bless the people here within,
> Keep them pure and free from sin;
> Bless us all that we may be
> Fit, O Lord, to dwell with thee.[1]

[1] Reproduced by permission of Boosey and Hawkes Ltd.

BREATHE ON ME, BREATH OF GOD

Edwin Hatch

THIS hymn is a genuine transatlantic one, for Edwin Hatch spent eight most memorable years in Canada, first as professor of classics in Trinity College, Toronto, and then as rector of the High School of Quebec.

Those years from 1859 to 1867 were a young man's years in Canada, and the peace and beauty of lakes and rivers must have had their effect on the sensitive spirit of Edwin Hatch. His later years in Oxford brought him honour and fame as church historian and theologian.

It was after his death in 1889 that his little book of poems *Towards Fields of Light* was published containing this little gem of prayer to the God the Holy Spirit:

> Breathe on me, Breath of God,
> Fill me with life anew,
> That I may love what Thou dost love,
> And do what Thou wouldst do.

It has the shape and light of genuine religious poetry. It lifts naturally,

> Breathe on me, Breath of God,
> Till I am wholly Thine,
> Until this earthly part of me
> Glows with Thy fire divine,

and soars to eternity,

> Breathe on me, Breath of God,
> So shall I never die,
> But live with Thee the perfect life
> Of Thine eternity.

BY COOL SILOAM'S SHADY RILL

Reginald Heber

AUSTRALIA and Canada evidently still love Heber's children's hymn which had such a vogue in Victorian days. It was published after his sad and sudden death in 1826 (*see* p. 33) with "rill" instead of "fountain" in the first line.

Siloam's lily and Sharon's rose were "Bible flowers" which blossomed in Heber's English garden, and he skilfully plants them into his hymn for youth. The hymn is now nearly always omitted from modern collections in Britain. Perhaps it is not valiant and stern enough. But its freshness and charm as a prayer and hope for youth still last on.

Heber's meditation on the lily and the rose was apt and not overdrawn,

> By cool Siloam's shady rill
>   The lily must decay;
> The rose that blooms beneath the hill
>   Must shortly fade away.

He then moves on to "man's maturer age", and finishes with a verse that gathers all the experiences of life together,

> Dependent on Thy bounteous breath,
>   We seek Thy grace alone,
> In childhood, manhood, age and death
>   To keep us still Thine own.

DEAR LORD AND FATHER OF MANKIND

John Greenleaf Whittier

No hymn that has come out of the life of the American people is better loved than this one. And yet Whittier was no hymn-lover, for he was a Quaker, and always stuck closely to the meetings of the Quakers where silent worship was strictly observed.

He once admitted, "I am not really a hymn-writer, for the very good reason that I know nothing of music. Only a few of my pieces were written for singing. A good hymn is the best use to which poetry can be devoted, but I do not claim that I have succeeded in composing one."

Whittier was eighty-five when he died in 1892, and most of his life was spent in the small towns of New England where he was a journalist and editor, and the verses which make up this hymn come from the poem *The Brewing of Soma*. This poem was Whittier's comment on some rather noisy revivalistic meetings in his neighbourhood. Whittier's somewhat rational approach to religion (more of his hymns were included in the hymn-book prepared for the Parliament of Religions in Chicago 1893 than of any other single writer) was offended by the wild goings on at this revival. He likened them to the brewing of the intoxicating African drink Soma which was supposed to excite religious feeling,

> And yet the past comes round again,
>   And new doth old fulfil;
> In sensual transports wild as vain
> We brew in many a Christian fane
>   The heathen Soma still.

Then in the next stanza follows the line *Dear Lord and*

Father which the English hymnologist, Garrett Horder, first used separately as a hymn in 1884.

> Dear Lord and Father of mankind,
>   Forgive our foolish ways;
> Reclothe us in our rightful mind;
> In purer lives Thy service find,
>   In deeper reverence praise.
>
> Breathe through the pulses of desire
>   Thy coolness and Thy balm;
> Let sense be dumb, its heats expire:
> Speak through the earthquake, wind, and fire,
>   O still small voice of calm!

Nearly all Whittier's hymns are essentially poems first. He never imagined they would be sung, although no doubt he would be happy to know the comfort and also sound instruction they have brought to thousands.

GOD BE WITH YOU TILL WE MEET AGAIN

Jeremiah Eames Rankin

THIS tenderly emotional hymn has gone round the English speaking world since Jeremiah Eames Rankin wrote it in 1882. He says he tried to write a hymn which was a Christian "Good-bye", for the common farewell, "Good-bye", is of course a contraction of the Christian salutation "God be with you" like the German "Grüss Gott".

So "God be with you till we meet again" is "Good-bye until we meet again". Looked at with this meaning in the mind, much of the sentimental and somewhat tearful attitude of the hymn is put into its rightful place.

Rankin himself was a New England Congregational minister, and perhaps some of the wide popularity of his hymn is due to the tune that William G. Tomer composed for it. The story goes that Rankin invited two composers to set a tune—one famous and the other unknown. He chose the unknown composer's work, and ever since hymn and tune have been more permanently wedded than most hymns and tunes.

Never was the hymn more fervently sung than at the morning service in the country church of Sandringham on November 15, 1953, when Queen Elizabeth and the Duke of Edinburgh were worshipping prior to their Commonwealth tour.

When the refrain, however, is sung the hymn changes its meaning to "Good-bye till we meet in heaven". Some hymnologists believe that the refrain was added by the composer, and was not part of Rankin's original version.

IN HEAVENLY LOVE ABIDING

Anna Laetitia Waring

ONE of the surprises about devotional verse of the mid-nineteenth century is the way in which it sold. Edition after edition of verse by writers who would not be accounted poets in the strict sense were bought up. Anna L. Waring's poems had that welcoming experience. At the age of thirty in 1850 she published her *Hymns and Meditations*, a small book of nineteen hymns which by 1863 had gone into ten editions, and contained thirty-eight hymns.

A Glamorganshire Welsh woman, her poems have the phrase and turn of one who not only had a genuine piety but knew how to express it. Four of her hymns have found permanent recognition: *My heart is resting O my God*, *Go not far from me O my strength*, *Father I know that all my life*, and *In heavenly love abiding*.

The nineteenth century would have voted for the first named as her best hymn, but the twentieth, judging by the popularity of its choice, goes for *In heavenly love abiding*. Not a robust or a bold hymn of discipleship, but one of calm and complete gospel assurance:

> Wherever He may guide me,
>   No want shall turn me back;
> My Shepherd is beside me,
>   And nothing can I lack:
>
> His wisdom ever waketh,
>   His sight is never dim;
> He knows the way He taketh,
>   And I will walk with Him.

SWEET HOUR OF PRAYER

W. W. Walford

> Sweet hour of pray'r
> That calls me from a world of care
> And bids me at my Father's throne
> Make all my wants and wishes known,
> In seasons of distress and grief
> My soul has often found relief,
> And oft escaped the tempter's snare
> By thy return, sweet hour of pray'r.

A MELODY, some easily memorized words, and the desire to sing together perhaps a little sentimentally, and maybe, a little tearfully—those are the happy ingredients of the "gospel song". It was the United States' own and dear invention.

The most successful practitioner of the "gospel song" was Fanny Crosby (1820–1915) who though blind had a genius for the gospel verse. Her verses were the glories of the Moody and Sankey revival meetings in the United States and in Britain, and have their place to-day. *Rescue the perishing* and *Safe in the Arms of Jesus* are Fanny Crosby's best known. But in the popular choices of radio congregations, however, none of them appear high up in the lists.

W. W. Walford, a blind preacher, about whom little is known, wrote this one "gospel song" in 1851 which stands high amongst United States choices.

How strong the "gospel song" choices are in the United States is shown by a poll of 10,000 people in Los Angeles by a local radio station on hymns. The order was:

The Old Rugged Cross (p. 142)
The Love of God

In the Garden (p. 125)
What a Friend we have in Jesus (p. 147)
Beyond the Sunset
Precious Lord take my hand
Rock of Ages (p. 139)
It is no Secret
Abide with me (p. 54)
No one ever cared for me like Jesus

Another poll conducted by the *Christian Herald* of New York resulted in this list,

The Old Rugged Cross
In the Garden
Nearer my God to Thee
What a Friend we have in Jesus
Sweet Hour of Prayer
Abide with me
I Love to Tell the Story
Rock of Ages
Jesus Lover of My Soul
He leadeth me

These choices are a significant commentary not only on taste in hymns but on popular religion too.

3

HYMNS OF EXPERIENCE

HYMNS OF EXPERIENCE

J. M. NEALE	*Art thou weary, art thou languid*
E. C. CLEPHANE	*Beneath the Cross of Jesus*
K. VON SCHLEGEL	*Be still my soul*
ISAAC WILLIAMS	*Be Thou my guardian and my guide*
F. W. FABER	*Faith of our fathers*
	Hark, hark, my soul
ROBERT MURRAY	*From ocean to ocean*
A. C. AINGER	*God is working His purpose out*
WILLIAM COWPER	*God moves in a mysterious way*
R. KIPLING	*God of our fathers*
W. WILLIAMS	*Guide me O Thou great Jehovah*
RICHARD KEEN	*How firm a foundation*
S. F. BENNETT	*In the sweet by and by*
J. H. NEWMAN	*Lead kindly light*
J. EDMESTON	*Lead us heavenly Father lead us*
S. F. ADAMS	*Nearer, my God, to Thee*
J. KEBLE	*New every morning is the love*
S. BARING-GOULD	*Now the day is over*
P. DODDRIDGE	*O God of Bethel*
G. MATHESON	*O love that wilt not let me go*
W. GLADDEN	*O Master let me walk with Thee*
ISAAC WATTS	*Our God our help in ages past*
F. R. HAVERGAL	*Take my life and let it be*
J. ELLERTON	*The day Thou gavest*
	Saviour again to Thy dear name
H. W. BAKER	*The king of love my shepherd is*
PSALM 23	*The Lord's my shepherd*
E. H. PLUMPTRE	*Thy hand, O God, has guided*

HYMNS OF EXPERIENCE

It is not surprising that a large group of hymns comes under this heading, for many hymns have been written out of some experience, or out of an incident in the author's life. This is the way that genuine emotion and piety are captured in a few verses.

This group of hymns contains some of the most loved and most sung hymns in the English language, such as *Our God our help in ages past*, *Guide Me O Thou great Jehovah*, *Lead Kindly Light*, *The Day Thou Gavest* and *Psalm 23*. But there are also some choices which are not so universally well-known.

Some of the favourites of the "gospel song" tradition come into this section, such as *In the sweet by and by*, and *Beneath the Cross of Jesus*. Also included here is a national hymn, Canada's much loved *From Ocean to Ocean*.

Christian experience is never of one pattern, and is always expressed differently from people to people in various parts of the world, but underlying it are the same deep themes of the Christian faith which are very clearly shown in this group of hymns.

ART THOU WEARY, ART THOU LANGUID?

J. M. Neale

A POOR hymn to begin with? No, one of the finest in the English tongue, and written by one to whom all hymn-lovers are in debt.

John Mason Neale probably got his inspiration for it from his intimate knowledge of Greek and Latin hymn-writers (*see* p. 148), but Neale's own skill and piety help to make the hymn. See how the hymn soars to its final grand conclusion,

> Finding, following, keeping, struggling,
>   Is He sure to bless?
> Saints, apostles, prophets, martyrs,
>   Answer, Yes!

That verse springs to one's mind when looking round the humble house for old people at East Grinstead in the English county of Sussex, where J. M. Neale was Warden for twenty years from 1846 to 1866. There for a few pounds a year he cared for a handful of elderly folk, wrote his hymns, did his translations, and founded the neighbouring sisterhood of St. Margaret's. As a holy man of religion, and scholar too, Neale never had a prominent place in the English church, for his "high church" views were frowned upon. But like the last verse of this hymn he knew the secret of "finding, following".

He was once on a visit to John Keble, author of *Sun of my Soul thou Saviour dear*, who was then compiling a hymn-book. For a few minutes Keble was out of the room looking up a reference, and when he returned Neale said that he thought all Keble's hymns were original and Keble agreed. "Look at this," said Neale producing a Latin version of one of Keble's poems.

Astonished to see it Keble protested that he had never seen it before, and was distressed to think that Neale should suspect his honesty. An awkward situation turned to laughter when Neale said that in Keble's absence from the room he had turned his English into Latin!

At the foot of scores of hymns Neale's name is prefixed *Tr. by*, a sign not only of his skill, and his familiarity with the Latin and Greek hymn-writers, but also of his own humility. He was happy to introduce the others— a pilgrim like his hymn,

> O happy band of pilgrims,
> If onward ye will tread,
> With Jesus as your fellow,
> To Jesus as your Head!

We owe him three of the hymns amongst the popular hundred: *Art Thou Weary, Jerusalem the Golden* (p. 126), *Ye Sons and Daughters* (p. 148), a number exceeded only by Charles Wesley himself.

BENEATH THE CROSS OF JESUS

Elizabeth Cecilia Clephane

How many summer visitors from the English speaking lands to the Scottish border associate a hymn-writer with the pleasant old town of Melrose, just three miles from Scott's Abbotsford? Elizabeth Clephane lived there within sight of the Abbey until she died in 1869 at the early age of 39. Australia and Canada both ask for her hymn,

> Beneath the Cross of Jesus
>   I fain would take my stand—
> The shadow of a mighty Rock,
>   Within a weary land;
> A home within the wilderness,
>   A rest upon the way,
> From the burning of the noon-tide heat,
>   And the burden of the day.

Those who look for the tang of the Border country will probably find it in her better known

> There were ninety and nine that safely lay
>   In the shelter of the fold;
> But one was out on the hills away,
>   Far off from the gates of gold,
> Away on the mountains wild and bare,
> Away from the tender Shepherd's care,

a hymn which Ira D. Sankey made so widely known in his evangelistic campaigns.

BE STILL MY SOUL

Katharina von Schlegel

VERY little is known of the origins of this hymn or of its author. Katharina von Schlegel, born in 1697, was probably head of a Women's House of the Evangelical Lutheran Church at Cöthen in Germany. She was also probably associated with the little ducal court of Cöthen. Her hymn was discovered and translated by Jane L. Borthwick (1813–97), and its popularity to-day is no doubt due to its setting to Sibelius' famous melody *Finlandia*. The *Church Hymnary* (1927) of the Presbyterian Churches of the British Commonwealth is the chief modern hymn-book to print it, and gives *Finlandia* as one of the two suggested tunes.

The hymn is an expression of deep piety and trust in God, a fine example of the German pietistic experience.

Be still, my soul: the Lord is on thy side;
   Bear patiently the cross of grief or pain;
Leave to thy God to order and provide;
   In every change He faithful will remain.
Be still, my soul: thy best, thy heavenly Friend
Through thorny ways leads to a joyful end.

Be still, my soul: thy God doth undertake
   To guide the future as He has the past.
Thy hope, thy confidence let nothing shake;
   All now mysterious shall be bright at last.
Be still, my soul: the waves and winds still know
His voice who ruled them while He dwelt below.

BE THOU MY GUARDIAN AND MY GUIDE

Isaac Williams

FOR those who know the story of Isaac Williams this hymn of his must always bring back memories of the warm and mellow countryside of England's Cotswolds and of Oxford. For Isaac Williams was one of that group of accomplished men of whom Keble, Newman and Froude were the leaders who in the early nineteenth century brought new life to the English church.

John Keble (*see* p. 92) was Isaac Williams' intimate friend. They lived together at Southrop on vacations from Oxford, and when Isaac went as curate to lovely Windrush in the Cotswold country near Oxford he was only twelve miles away from Keble at equally lovely Fairford.

Learning at Oxford, and meditative loveliness in the country, were the background of Isaac Williams' life. He might have been Professor of Poetry at Oxford, following Keble, but for his old association with J. H. Newman whose curate he had been at St. Mary's. That killed his chances.

So he withdrew even more deeply into the Cotswold country and spent the last seventeen years of his life at Stinchcombe. His hymn has all the quality of personal religion, and is perhaps first a poem and second a hymn.

> And if I tempted am to sin,
>   And outward things are strong,
> Do Thou, O Lord, keep watch within,
>   And save my soul from wrong.

FAITH OF OUR FATHERS

F. W. Faber

THIS popular hymn of F. W. Faber's owes its popularity chiefly to its use in North America. It is often sung in the United States alongside *My Country 'tis of thee* perhaps with little knowledge of why Faber wrote the hymn.

Faber, who had been an Anglican clergyman, wrote all his hymns after being received into the Roman Catholic Church in 1846. He then went to a school in the English county of Staffordshire, and afterwards, in 1854, to the Brompton Oratory in London—a famous preaching centre of the Roman Catholic Church.

Faber, of course, was always anxious to maintain his view that the true Church in England was continued through the Roman Catholic Church; that was "the faith of our fathers" he wrote his hymn about. But hymns have a habit of becoming bigger than their authors, and Faber's hymn is sung fervently by Protestants as well as Roman Catholics. It is another example of the universality of hymns, and their knack of overstepping the boundaries which divide Christians.

While his other hymns such as *Souls of men why will ye scatter* will be more universally known (*see* p. 78) this one is a rare sample of how a hymn can preserve a bit of sound history. Faber's lines:

> Faith of our Fathers living still
> In spite of dungeon, fire and sword

are a recognition by the hymn singer that religious intolerance was not confined to one side only. Faber did perhaps more than he intended with this hymn, which deserves to be included more often in all English language hymn-books.

FROM OCEAN TO OCEAN

Robert Murray

CANADA's national hymn owes its origin to Robert Murray, a Presbyterian minister in the Maritime Provinces, and later editor of the church paper *The Presbyterian Witness*. Murray had a touch of celtic imagination from his Scottish ancestry, and caught a vision of Canada stretching from ocean to ocean,

> From ocean unto ocean
>   Our land shall own Thee, Lord,
> And filled with true devotion
>   Obey Thy sovereign word.
>
> Our prairies and our mountains,
>   Forest and fertile field,
> Our rivers, lakes and fountains
>   To Thee shall tribute yield,

a hope that has given the hymn a sure place in Canada's affection.

Murray also most happily added a verse to the national anthem *God Save the Queen*,

> Our loved Dominion bless,
> With peace and happiness
>   From shore to shore;
> And let our Empire be
> United, loyal, free,
> True to herself and Thee
>   For evermore.

79

GOD IS WORKING HIS PURPOSE OUT

A. C. Ainger

No place in England is more visited by English speaking peoples than the twin towns of Windsor and Eton lying opposite one another on the Thames, one famous for its castle, home of the reigning sovereign, and the other for its college where hundreds of famous Englishmen have been schooled.

At Eton for nearly fifty years Arthur Campbell Ainger lived as boy and master. Eton owes to him many of its celebrated songs including its *Founder's Day Hymn for King Henry VI*,

> Praise the Lord! to-day we sing,
> Birthday of our Founder King!
> Day of memories! linking fast
> With the present all the past!
> For the royal care that planned
> God's own house, wherein we stand,
> Lift your hearts with one accord,
> Lift your hearts, and praise the Lord!

and he wrote this fine hymn:

> God is working His purpose out as year succeeds to year;
> God is working His purpose out and the time is drawing near;
> Nearer and nearer draws the time, the time that shall surely be,
> When the earth shall be filled with the glory of God as the waters cover the sea.

His stately, vigorous hymn has all the "go" in it that boys like, and it must have made a "noble noise" in Eton College chapel with a thousand boys' clear voices. The last two lines of each verse, *When the earth shall be filled with the glory of God as the waters cover the sea* are woven in triumphantly from Isaiah 11: 9.

GOD MOVES IN A MYSTERIOUS WAY

William Cowper

THE little town of Olney in Buckinghamshire is famous nowadays for the pancake race which the women of the town race each year against the women of Liberal, Kansas, U.S.A.

Down the end of the street where the women race, not far from the church and the River Ouse, is a modest red brick house where the author of this hymn lived for nineteen years, leaving it in 1786 for one only a mile or two away on the hill at Weston Underwood. It is a gloomy little house and must have often depressed William Cowper who was so easily depressed.

In a fit of depression which later turned towards suicide, Cowper was moved to write,

> Ye fearful saints, fresh courage take:
> The clouds ye so much dread
> Are big with mercy, and shall break
> In blessings on your head.

His friend John Newton, another hymn-writer, who was Vicar of Olney, cared for Cowper, and together they wrote many hymns for the congregation to sing. Their book *Olney Hymns* has some of the most loved hymns, *How sweet the name of Jesus* by Newton, and Cowper's *Hark my soul*.

Between Cowper's house and the vicarage garden a little doorway was made for the friends to go to and fro, and on Wednesday evenings Newton's prayer meeting always included Cowper, the one-time sailor in a slave ship who became a parson kneeling with the often half-crazy poet who wrote some of the best remembered lines in the English language. In the Oxford *Dictionary of Quotations* there are twelve columns of popular quotations from Cowper, which is some indication of the genius that once lived in sleepy Olney.

Amongst the quotations is the whole of this hymn except two lines, and eighteen other verses from Cowper's hymns. Cowper could also strike off memorable lines which have entered familiar English speech, such as

God made the country, and man made the town

and,

Who loves a garden loves a greenhouse too

and those four lines,

> I am monarch of all I survey,
>   My right there is none to dispute;
> From the centre all round to the sea
>   I am lord of the fowl and the brute.

GOD OF OUR FATHERS, KNOWN OF OLD

Rudyard Kipling

A PLACE of pilgrimage for many visitors from over-
seas to Britain is a house in a valley in the village of
Burwash in the South Downs. It is called Bateman's
and the date over the doorway is 1634, and the house
was built by one who worked in the local iron trade in
the days when rural England wrought its own iron
tools and equipment.

Bateman's has all the solid look of comfortable pros-
perity, and its most famous owner—Rudyard Kipling—
added to it during the thirty-four years he lived there until
his death in 1936. The terraces, lawns, yew hedges and rose
garden are his, a bit of the beauty he added to the English
scene in addition to the stories and poems he wrote.

It would have pleased him to know that in the
popular choices of hymns Canada gives a place to his
Recessional, which he wrote at the height of the "pomp
and circumstance" of the British Empire in 1897 at
Queen Victoria's Diamond Jubilee. He thought that
this with his *Just So Stories* would last on in literature.

It may be that with the "passing of empire" Kipling's
verse, which celebrated the majesty and splendour of a
"far-flung battle line", and spoke of "lesser breeds without the law", is out-dated. But there is something very
deeply moving in this hymn which recognizes the faults
as well as the virtues of the empire builders of whom
Kipling was proud from the days of his youth in India,

> For frantic boast and foolish word—
> Thy mercy on Thy people, Lord.

Kipling was the grandson of Joseph Kipling, a Methodist minister, and his wife Alice was the daughter of
G. B. Macdonald, a Methodist minister. John Wesley

himself called Alice's grandfather, James Macdonald, to be a preacher. Did not the gospel strain come out in Rudyard Kipling, the poet, too?

GUIDE ME O THOU GREAT JEHOVAH
"Arglwydd, arwain trwy'r anialwch"

William Williams

As the traveller by road from London enters Cambridge by Trumpington village a glance to the right as he passes the end of the Botanical Gardens will show the modest, but beautiful, range of buildings of Cheshunt College. If he should walk into the dining-hall he will see over the mantelpiece Romney's portrait of the college founder, Selina, Countess of Huntingdon, who in 1785 began to train "godly and pious young men" for the Christian ministry.

The Countess always had an eye for doing things in the proper manner, and her college—then at Trevecca in South Wales—had Wales's "sweet singer", William Williams, to celebrate its opening with a new hymn. So *Arglwydd, arwain trwy'r anialwch* was born, and has since become a firm favourite wherever hymns are sung.

Its third verse *When I tread the verge of Jordan* has a line *Land me safe on Canaan's side* which was once printed in the United States as *Land my safe on Canaan's side*. The delighted discoverer of the illuminating misprint commented "No, you can't take it with you, brother".

The hymn's imagery is well matched by the powerful glow of the tune "Cwm Rhondda" which Wales has made the world sing to this great hymn.

HOW FIRM A FOUNDATION

Richard Keen

FEW passages of Scripture have been more aptly put into verse than the first five verses of Isaiah 43 as they appear in this hymn. But who was Richard Keen with the date 1787 appended to his name? Prolonged enquiry by the hymn experts over the years have failed to discover who he was. Amongst the hundred hymns discussed in this book here is the "anonymous" author at last! Was he really *Keith* or was he *Kirkham*? His legacy to the English singing people is a noble one, and his firm, stately lines have all the Biblical majesty about them:

> When through fiery trials thy pathway shall lie,
> His grace all-sufficient shall be thy supply;
> The flame shall not hurt thee, His only design
> Thy dross to consume and thy gold to refine.

And then the unknown Richard moves away beyond Isaiah, and puts a triumphant conclusion to his hymn,

> The soul that on Jesus has leaned for repose
> He will not, He cannot, desert to its foes;
> That soul, though all hell should endeavour to shake,
> He never will leave, He will never forsake.

Keen's original last line was even more emphatic, *He'll never, no never, no never forsake.*

IN THE SWEET BY AND BY

Samuel Fillmore Bennett

THIS gospel song, famed for its chorus,

> In the sweet by and by
> We shall meet on that beautiful shore,

is a genuine product of the mid-west of the United States, and jumped into life as the result of a chance conversation between Samuel Fillmore Bennett and his musician friend, Joseph P. Webster, in Elkhorn, Wis., in the years of the gospel song makers in the mid-nineteenth century.

Webster came into Bennett's office one day looking depressed and when Bennett asked him what was the matter he replied that "It would be all right by and by". That phrase leaped into life for Bennett. "The sweet by and by," he mused, "that would make a good hymn." There and then he started to write the verse,

> There's a land that is fairer than day,
> And by faith we can see it afar,
> For the Father waits over the way
> To prepare us a dwelling place there.

Webster caught his friend's enthusiasm, and hummed out a melody, and bringing in a friend with his violin the three men were soon singing the song.

> We shall sing on that beautiful shore
> The melodious songs of the blest,
> And our spirits shall sorrow no more,
> Not a sigh for the blessing of rest.

The Salvation Army have popularized the song, and *In the sweet by and by* is often sung at Army funeral services.

LEAD KINDLY LIGHT

John Henry Newman

WHEN he was a young man of thirty J. H. Newman did what many young men of his day had done before him —set off on a tour of Europe. From Naples he sailed over to Sicily with a supply of "curry powder, spice, pepper, salt, sugar, tea and ham; cold cream, a straw hat, and a map of Sicily. I shall want nothing from the island", he wrote, "but macaroni, honey and eggs."

In Sicily he fell ill. The horrible beds, the fleas, the heat, the bad food and an incompetent doctor brought Newman to death's door. At least he thought he might die. His mind roamed over his past life, his sins, "my utter hollowness". He was homesick. "I sat", he says, "sometime by the bedside crying bitterly, and all I could say was that I was sure God had some work for me to do in England."

He gradually got better. He called a cup of tea "life from the dead", and loved the aloes by the roadside, and the scent of camomile flowers. The grandeur of Etna made him write, "It was worth coming all the way, to endure sadness, loneliness, weariness to see it. . . . I felt that I should be a better and more religious man if I lived there."

At last, aching to get home, he got on board an orange boat bound for Marseilles. It was a weary, slow voyage and in the straits between Sardinia and Corsica they were becalmed for a week. There between the two islands Newman got out pen and paper and wrote *Lead kindly Light*—the poem of a homesick traveller which the genius of Newman turned into a religious experience that has comforted and inspired thousands. It is one of the three hymns which are always chosen whenever hymns come up for judgment.

LEAD US HEAVENLY FATHER LEAD US

James Edmeston

In the Canadian selection of hymns this one of James Edmeston's bears an unfamiliar author's name. Finding out about him took me on a London bus down through the East End to Homerton where he lived and worked for over fifty years until his death in 1867.

The Homerton Edmeston knew was a retired and leafy suburb of well-built eighteenth century houses, little squares of brick houses all long since turned into tenements and flats. Some of Hitler's bombs left wide holes in Homerton, but long before that happened Homerton's peace had dissolved into the noise and bustle of London.

Edmeston was an architect, but his hymn-writing facility was so marked that he published over two thousand hymns, and is said to have written one a week for family worship. The names of his collections— *For the Assistance of Cottagers in their Domestic Worship*, *Hymns for the Chamber of Sickness*, and *Infant Breathings*, *Hymns for the Young*—indicate his general style. And out of all that comes this fine hymn, *Lead us Heavenly Father*, with many easily remembered lines in it such as "O'er the world's tempestuous sea" and

> Thus provided, pardoned, guided,
> Nothing can our peace destroy.

One likes to think of Edmeston, the industrious architect, and churchwarden of St. Barnabas, Homerton, working at his blue-prints, and his hymns, perhaps at the same time. One of his pupils was Giles Gilbert Scott whose grandson designed Liverpool Cathedral— England's most notable modern cathedral, a rare hymn in stone.

NEARER, MY GOD, TO THEE

Sarah Flower Adams

FEW hymns have been sung in more tragic circumstances than this one on the night of April 14, 1912, on board the sinking *Titanic*. The great ship, at that time the greatest in the world, was on its maiden voyage to New York with a happy, expectant company of over two thousand people including many famous ones. Shortly before midnight, on the third day on the Atlantic, as the evening parties on the ship were breaking up, the ship shuddered from stem to stern. The lights, however, still blazed, the band played, and while the passengers turned to one another with anxious looks none of them doubted that all was well.

The alarms rang through the ship, and within a few minutes passengers were standing on deck with their life-belts knowing that the ship had struck an iceberg, and that the sea was pouring into a vast rent down below. The supply of life-belts and life-boats proved inadequate, and while the great ship listed heavily towards her doom alternate waves of fear and calm spread through the passengers lining the decks. It was then that the band played the tune of *Nearer my God to Thee*, and the passengers, all of whom were looking death in the face, sang

> E'en though it be a cross
>   That raiseth me,
> Still all my song shall be
> Nearer, my God, to Thee.

In three hours the *Titanic* went down into the icy Atlantic, and only seven hundred and eleven lives were saved.

Sarah Flower Adams was a young woman of forty-three when she died in 1848, and her home was at Harlow in the English county of Essex. Her hymns are more widely used in America than elsewhere, particularly amongst Unitarians.

Nearer my God to Thee is based on Jacob's dream (Gen. 28: 12) in which the ladder, set up on earth, reaches to heaven, a vision which the writer deftly weaves into her hymn:

> There let the way appear,
>   Steps unto heaven;
> All that Thou sendest me
>   In mercy given:
> Angels to beckon me
> Nearer, my God, to Thee,
>   Nearer to Thee!
>
> Then, with my waking thoughts
>   Bright with Thy praise,
> Out of my stony griefs
>   Bethel I'll raise;
> So by my woes to be
> Nearer, my God, to Thee,
>   Nearer to Thee!

NEW EVERY MORNING IS THE LOVE

John Keble

THE traveller who goes by road from London to Southampton, on his way perhaps to the United States or Canada, passes through the village of Hursley. He should stop and go into the churchyard and look for the graves of John and Charlotte Keble who lived in the vicarage for thirty years from 1836 to 1866. The church itself was built out of the money John Keble earned chiefly from the sale of his popular *Christian Year*. John Keble had one of the loveliest faces, so his friends said, that ever graced a man, and his still lovelier spirit shines in his hymns.

It is surprising that the choice of hymn-listeners does not fall on his *Sun of my Soul, Thou Saviour dear*, the evening hymn which comes into most books. But it seems that it is Keble's morning hymn that is the most popular. Keble's first verse began "O timely happy, timely wise", but familiar use has given the hymn its name as *New every morning*.

Keble was still under nineteen when he was elected a Fellow of Oriel College, Oxford, and he passed all his life in that mellow countryside which lies between his native town of Fairford in the Cotswolds and the Hampshire village of Hursley. Something of the green loveliness of it all is in the poems, because they are poems first and hymns afterwards. He never went to school, for his father taught him and his brother, and the years of his life were prosperous and pleasant.

But Keble wrote as if he knew of the rougher side of life:

> Old friends, old scenes, will lovelier be
> As more of heaven in each we see:

Some softening gleam of love and prayer
Shall dawn on every cross and care.

It is worth going into the National Portrait Gallery in London's Trafalgar Square to look at Keble's saintly face, and that of his friend J. H. Newman near it.

Both men were baptized deeply into the Christian faith. They show it in their hymns as well as in their faces. Divided by church loyalties yet both were united in the centralities of the faith which had its fixed spots not on earth but in heaven,

Only, O Lord, in Thy dear love
Fit us for perfect rest above;
And help us, this and every day,
To live more nearly as we pray.

NOW THE DAY IS OVER

S. Baring-Gould

It was while Sabine Baring-Gould was a young curate at Horbury Brig (*see also* p. 156) in the Calder valley of Yorkshire in 1865 that he wrote this hymn.

He lived in a small cottage with a single room on the ground-floor, a back-kitchen, and one single room above. In the room he used to hold a night school and the bedroom above was made into a little chapel. In his *Reminiscences* he says,

> I began with night school every evening in the winter and with service every Sunday evening in the chapel. I had to stand on a stool before the chimney piece, on which was stood a cross and a pair of candlesticks. I wore no surplice, only a cassock. Very soon a congregation was formed, that grew till it not only filled the upper room, but occupied the stairs as well, and the kitchen below. Hymns were performed somewhat laggingly, as the singing had to bump down the stairs, fill the kitchen, and one strain of the tune after another came up irregularly through the chinks in the floor, to interfere with the smoothness and sequence of the melody as sung above. The notes from the stairs also jostled.

It was before the days of education for all, and "night schools" such as Baring-Gould's were all that working people and their children had. After school the boys and girls (who had probably done a long day's work in the woollen mills) egged him on to tell them a story. They held him by his coat-lapels, "You mun tell us a tale afore you go," and Baring-Gould would begin, "Once upon a time", with all the ready invention that he used for his tales of his native Devonshire in after years.

It was for his Yorkshire "night school" that Baring-Gould wrote his lovely evening hymn with the singing bumping "down the stairs" and into the kitchen, and out into the cold, sharp air of the Calder valley.

> Now the darkness gathers,
>   Stars begin to peep,
> Birds and beasts and flowers
>   Soon will be asleep.
>
> Grant to little children
>   Visions bright of Thee:
> Guard the sailors tossing
>   On the deep blue sea.
>
> When the morning wakens,
>   Then may I arise
> Pure, and fresh, and sinless
>   In Thy holy eyes.

O GOD OF BETHEL

Philip Doddridge

THIS famous hymn takes us into midland England, to the boot and shoe making town of Northampton where in 1730 Philip Doddridge began his ministry of twenty-one years.

Most likely the hymn arose out of a sermon based on Genesis 28: 20–22 for Doddridge had an original way with his congregations. At the end of a sermon he would recite a hymn connected with it, and get his congregation to repeat it line by line. Few of them, of course, could read and write so a hymn-book would not have been very helpful. One member of his church, however, did copy down the Doddridge hymns, over five hundred of them. This hymn has been re-written first by John Logan and then by the Scottish Paraphrases of 1781.

Doddridge himself was only forty-nine when he died in 1751 but his Northampton ministry set a standard of piety and thoroughness for the ministry of the Free Churches in England.

He was a friend of Isaac Watts and this hymn is a close companion to *Our God our help in ages past*. Both men were not only pioneers in hymn-writing, but they realized that worshippers would naturally make hymns their prayers and meditations at the same time. In fact they were authors of "prayer-books" as much as hymn-books, although neither of them set out consciously to make a hymn-book.

O LOVE THAT WILT NOT LET ME GO

George Matheson

"Doon the wa'er"—for any Scotsman means a trip down the lovely Firth of Clyde from Glasgow and out to the broader waters that lap the coast of Arran.

All the stopping places for the steamers have their associations and their own special beauty—Kilcraggan, Kilmun, Dunoon, Wemyss Bay, Rothesay, and little Innellan. Just at the point where the Firth begins to widen into a sea loch Innellan stands. It is a memorable beauty spot in summer, and it once had for its parish minister George Matheson, the author of this poignantly beautiful hymn.

George Matheson was blind from childhood. But his student days in Edinburgh, where he graduated in 1862, were brilliant in academic achievement. It was on a summer evening in 1882 at Innellan that he had the sudden inspiration to write the hymn under the stress of a deep personal bereavement. He was in the Manse, and said afterwards that the hymn was composed in only a few minutes. At least it seemed like that to Matheson who said that he was in "mental distress" and that the hymn was "the fruit of pain".

It is one of the most personal hymns in the English tongue, and has ministered to the triumphant sorrow of many thousands.

> I lay in dust life's glory dead,
> And from the ground there blossoms **red**
> Life that shall endless be.

O MASTER LET ME WALK WITH THEE

Washington Gladden

MANY good hymns have not been written as hymns. This is one of them. Washington Gladden was a Congregational minister in Massachusetts and New York, and while there he edited a magazine, *The Sunday Afternoon*. Just before he moved to Columbus, Ohio, in 1882 he wrote a poem for his magazine beginning with the lines:

> O Master let me walk with thee
> In lowly paths of service free.

The following year it was included in a hymn-book, *Songs of Christian Praise*, and has most happily gone round the world since then.

America calls it "a social service hymn", but one British hymn-book most aptly puts it under the heading of "the love and service of man". It has the piety of personal religion, but also a concern for the "Christian mission" to "the slow of heart" and "the wayward feet".

Four years before it was written a boy was born in England in 1875 with the name of Gilbert Keith Chesterton who later wrote,

> O God of earth and altar,
>   Bow down and hear our cry,
> Our earthly rulers falter,
>   Our people drift and die.

Both hymn-writers were preaching a "social gospel". Gladden spoke to his American generation, and Chesterton to his British generation, and both hymns win a response to-day, because they have, what a good hymn must always have, a personal gospel.

OUR GOD OUR HELP IN AGES PAST

Isaac Watts

THIS hymn has been called "The International Anthem". A paraphrase of Psalm 90, it is Isaac Watts' most stately hymn with all his sense of time, man's insignificance before God, and yet the close link between God and man,

> Under the shadow of Thy throne
> Thy saints have dwelt secure:
> Sufficient is Thine arm alone,
> And our defence is sure.

It is universal in its scope, and is sung wherever English hymns are sung.

In all the troubled years of the twentieth century this hymn has been used at the moments of crisis—particularly those of war.

I remember it being sung on board the *Queen Elizabeth* ploughing her way through the Atlantic black-out with thousands of young American G.I.s making for the Normandy beaches. I can hear it still in a London church on a hushed Sunday morning after a night of bombing. Round the war memorials on countless village greens, and in great cathedrals, Isaac Watts' anthem has spoken of the hopes and fears of mortal men in peril and deliverance.

Watts (*see* p. 30) was a modest, quiet man who for thirty-six years of his life, from 1712 to 1748, lived with his friends the Abneys. Sir Thomas Abney was Lord Mayor of London in 1700. It is said that his income was never more than £100 a year and he gave most of it away in charity. There is a memorial to him in Westminster Abbey and he is buried in Bunhill Fields—with Bunyan and Defoe.

A group of Oxford dons when asked by Jowett of Balliol which hymn they most esteemed put *Our God our help* before all the rest. This judgment is approved by all the world. *Our God our help* is one of the sure, safe hymns. Particularly it is successful in the open air with the town band confident about the familiar tune.

For those brought up in the years following the First World War, Watts' hymn belongs to the tapestry of the seasonal round, and more especially to raw days in winter standing by a war memorial. Watts gave it a title which deserves to be placed at the top of the hymn whenever it is printed: "Man Frail and God Eternal".

> A thousand ages in Thy sight
>   Are like an evening gone;
> Short as the watch that ends the night
>   Before the rising sun.

TAKE MY LIFE AND LET IT BE

Frances Ridley Havergal

THERE are few hymns in the English language with a more personal appeal than this one, and that was how Frances Ridley Havergal intended it to be. She was the daughter of a rector in Worcester, England, and in 1851 had a deep religious experience which left a permanent mark on her life. She wrote, "I committed my soul to the Saviour, and earth and heaven seemed brighter from that moment."

She sincerely reflected that experience in all her writing. During her brief lifetime—she died in 1879 aged forty-three—her verses were printed on little cards and widely sold as ornamental furbelows for the Victorian mantelpiece, bedroom and prayer-book and Bible. Her hymn *I am trusting Thee Lord Jesus* was her favourite and the lines were found in her Bible at her death.

She is too personal perhaps for wide popular choice, but the British Broadcasting Corporation list gives four choices of *Take my life* in two years. Verse four of the hymn has sometimes been charged with putting hypocrisy on the lips of the singer,

> Take my silver and my gold,
> Not a mite would I withhold;
> Take my intellect, and use
> Every power as Thou shalt choose.

But whenever that verse is sung the singer is faced with that personal challenge of the stewardship of resources, which is what the writer hoped for. She wrote the hymn in February 1874 while on a visit to friends. Late one night she went to two of the girls in the house who were "troubled in soul" and helped them to "trust and rejoice". Miss Havergal was too happy to sleep and passed most of the night in prayer. She found the couplets of this hymn forming in her mind and leading up to the last line, "Ever only *all* for Thee".

> Take my will, and make it Thine;
> It shall be no longer mine;
> Take my heart, it is Thine own;
> It shall be Thy royal throne.
>
> Take my love, my Lord, I pour
> At Thy feet its treasure-store;
> Take myself, and I will be
> Ever, only, all for Thee.

Never have the tender demands of Christ been more directly put in a hymn. Every line is an appeal demanding a response.

THE DAY THOU GAVEST
SAVIOUR, AGAIN TO THY DEAR NAME WE RAISE

John Ellerton

JOHN ELLERTON'S two hymns have been brought together because they are partners in most hymn-books although the first one was not written as an evening hymn. Ellerton wrote it in 1870 for a liturgy for missionary meetings. Queen Victoria chose it as one of the hymns for her Diamond Jubilee in 1897 and so helped to establish its popularity.

Ellerton was a scholarly clergyman who could produce good hymns, as it were, to order. He wrote one for a choir festival, another for the wedding of the Duke of Westminster's daughter, one for the consecration of a burial ground, another for the re-opening of the nave of Chester Cathedral, and one for a flower service, and even one to comfort people in the bad harvest of 1881.

But these two hymns are probably his best known, particularly *The day Thou gavest*. There is an appealing spaciousness about it, and it gives a congregation a sense of fellowship with others round the world. Ellerton had the gift of making each line speak. It is a sensible, sincere hymn, and the singer finds himself singing what he believes, a sharp test of hymn-writing which Ellerton passes with high credit.

> So be it, Lord; Thy throne shall never
> Like earth's proud empires, pass away,
> Thy kingdom stands and grows for ever,
> Till all Thy creatures own Thy sway.

And in *Saviour, again* Ellerton most happily captures the peace of evening worship with a congregation kneeling for the blessing.

THE KING OF LOVE MY SHEPHERD IS

Henry Williams Baker

IF down the years the great Shepherd Psalm has been turned and twisted to suit the generations and their singing capacities, no one did it more happily than Sir Henry Williams Baker in this hymn. He devoted his life (1821–77) to hymns, and stayed for twenty-six years as vicar in the little village of Monkland amongst the apple orchards of England's Herefordshire in order that he might write hymns and edit hymn-books.

For years he worked on the first comprehensive hymn-book that was offered to the Church of England, which has won such a place of affection for itself, *Hymns Ancient and Modern*, and was himself a prolific contributor to it. *Hymns A and M* have gone along with the Bible and Prayer Book as part of the permanent equipment of the worshipper in the Anglican Church. The lettering *A and M* on the spine of the book once made a busy newspaper editor demand from his paper's library *Hymns N to Z*!

Baker's rendering of Psalm 23 is his monument. It has an easy swing about it that is missing from some of the artificialities of the metrical versions. Verse three is particularly expressive of the Good Shepherd,

> Perverse and foolish oft I strayed,
>   But yet in love He sought me,
> And on His shoulder gently laid,
>   And home, rejoicing, brought me.

These were the last words that Baker spoke as he lay dying—as tender a verse as any written in the hymn-books.

THE LORD'S MY SHEPHERD

Psalm 23

THE tale of this great and famous Psalm goes back to the days when Scotland became a land of the Reformation and turned its heart towards the Psalms.

For three hundred years and more the Scottish churches sang the Psalms in the metrical versions, and placed this Shepherd Psalm high amongst their favourites. It has often changed its face. For instance in 1641 its first verse went like this:

> My Shepheard is the living Lord,
>   and he that doth me feed;
> How can I then lack anything
>   whereof I stand in need.

Five years later the solemn divines of the Westminster Assembly changed it to this:

> The Lord my shepheard is, I shall
>   not want; he makes me ly
> In pastures green, me leads by streams
>   that do run quietly.

Every hymn-lover in every country where the Psalms are treasured has his memories of Psalm 23, and its link with the haunting melody *Crimond* has provided it with further popularity.

Queen Elizabeth chose the psalm-hymn for her marriage service, and whenever a group starts to sing in company Psalm 23 is bound to be chosen.

I remember it being sung on a Scottish hillside overlooking the Tummel where amongst the early heather the young Scottish voices passed naturally from *Ye Banks and Braes* to *The Lord's my Shepherd*—almost the national anthem of Scotland and full of tender memories and associations.

THY HAND, O GOD, HAS GUIDED

Edward Hayes Plumptre

It was in a small village in southern England where in the parish church a friend was being inducted as vicar that this fine hymn was first heard by the writer. The village street was lively with people, and the evening lights in the cottages were bright and friendly. The clear glass windows of the church were shining with light too, and a pool of light was about the church porch. Everybody and everything seemed ready to give the new vicar a welcome.

On such an occasion the first hymn is all-important. One looked at the unfamiliar words, and the name of the author whose reputation lay in the world of Biblical scholarship. *Thy hand, O God, has guided*—a trumpet start for a ministry! Then the organ played the tune, and a little procession came out of the vestry singing the hymn as a processional. The congregation seemed to shout the last line of each verse—"One Church, One Faith, One Lord".

Dean Plumptre's hymn has grown rapidly into a favoured position because of its happy combination of firm, clear lines, and a tune which a congregation can go for. He wrote it to defend the Church in the late nineteenth century, and by the Church meant the Church of England. But like all great hymns this one has been adopted by the Church Universal so that Christians of all communions sing it and in doing so affirm their belief in the Great Church.

This great hymn of the Church came out of the old cathedral city of Wells in England's county of Somerset. In the shadow of that beautiful building Dr. Plumptre lived for ten years as Dean. Its rare west front is crowded with the carved statues of prophets, kings, bishops, heroes, angels, martyrs and apostles. There are three hundred and fifty in all, arranged in eight horizontal tiers, all testifying to "the wondrous tale" of "the heralds" who "brought glad tidings". What Wells cathedral says in stone Dean Plumptre says in his hymn—"One Church, One Faith, One Lord".

Thy hand, O God, has guided
　　Thy flock, from age to age;
The wondrous tale is written,
　　Full clear, on every page;
Our fathers owned Thy goodness,
　　And we their deeds record;
And both of this bear witness,
　　One Church, One Faith, One Lord.

Thy heralds brought glad tidings
　　To greatest, as to least;
They bade men rise, and hasten
　　To share the great King's feast;
And this was all their teaching,
　　In every deed and word,
To all alike proclaiming
　　One Church, One Faith, One Lord.

HYMNS OF CHRIST, THE GOSPEL, AND THE CHURCH

EDWARD PERRONET — *All hail the power of Jesu's name*

JOHN FAWCETT — *Blest be the tie that binds*

BRIDGES AND THRING — *Crown Him with many crowns*

G. THRING — *Fierce raged the tempest*

JOHN NEWTON — *Glorious things of thee are spoken*
How sweet the name of Jesus sounds

HORATIUS BONAR — *I heard the voice of Jesus say*

ANNIE S. HAWKS — *I need Thee every hour*

JOHN OXENHAM — *In Christ there is no east or west*

C. AUSTIN MILES — *In the garden*

BERNARD OF CLUNY — *Jerusalem the golden*

CHRISTIAN GELLERT — *Jesus lives, thy terrors now*

CHARLES WESLEY — *Jesus lover of my soul*
Love divine all loves excelling
O for a thousand tongues to sing
O Thou who camest from above
Ye servants of God

ISAAC WATTS — *Jesus shall reign*
When I survey the wondrous Cross

BERNARD OF CLAIRVAUX — *Jesus Thou joy of loving hearts*
Jesus the very thought of Thee

E. W. SHURTLEFF — *Lead on O king eternal*

P. GERHARDT	*O sacred Head sore wounded*
H. AUBER	*Our blest Redeemer ere He breathed*
A. M. TOPLADY	*Rock of Ages*
WILL THOMPSON	*Softly and tenderly Jesus is calling*
S. J. STONE	*The Church's one foundation*
G. BENNARD	*The old rugged cross*
C. F. ALEXANDER	*There is a green hill*
	Jesus calls us o'er the tumult
E. S. ELLIOTT	*Thou didst leave Thy throne*
W. BULLOCK	*We love the place O God*
THOMAS KELLY	*We sing the praise of Him who died*
	The Head that once was crowned with thorns
J. SCRIVEN	*What a friend we have in Jesus*
tr. J. M. NEALE	*Ye sons and daughters of the king*

4

HYMNS OF CHRIST, THE GOSPEL, AND THE CHURCH

THIS section naturally contains some of the noblest hymns in the English language, for, as with all art inspired by the central acts of the Christian story, it is round Our Lord and His Church that much inspired hymn-writing gathers. Some of the masters are here too—Wesley, Watts, Newton, Thomas Kelly and Toplady.

Wesley's *Jesus Lover of my Soul* is in this section, and it seems appropriate to gather five of his great hymns together instead of dealing with them separately. Two of Watts's finest hymns come here too, and two of Newton's.

Radio audiences have chosen some thirty-six hymns under the general title of this section. That itself is a sign of how closely "popular" hymn samplers keep to the big and eternal themes of the faith, and do not stray far from it in their choices.

There is not a hymn in this section which does not "celebrate" Christ and the Gospel and the Church in a serious and non-sentimental fashion. There is little, if any, of what Mr. Bernard Manning in his *Hymns of Wesley and Watts* calls "metaphorical confectionery". True, there are hymns not to be found in the more orthodox hymn-books, such as *The Old Rugged Cross* and *Softly and Tenderly Jesus is Calling*, but that makes the collection all the richer.

ALL HAIL THE POWER OF JESU'S NAME

Edward Perronet

TWENTY miles south-east of London, below the first line of chalk hills which form the southern ramparts of Britain, lies the pretty village of Shoreham. A giant cross is scored on the hill facing the parish church, under whose roof Edward Perronet first knew "the power of Jesu's name". His father was vicar here from 1728 to 1785, and in the church there is a memorial to Vincent Perronet's long and holy ministry.

Wesley himself used to come over the downs on horse-back and along the Darent valley to visit Vincent, of whom he once wrote, "O that I may follow him in holiness". To the young Edward, John Wesley was hero, and he followed him on his journeys, once being thrown down and rolled in the mud by a crowd in Bolton, Lancashire. Like Timothy and Paul he was one of John Wesley's "sons in the gospel", but he parted from his master on the question of lay administration of the Sacraments, and eventually became the minister of an independent church in Canterbury.

Often called the "Coronation Hymn", Perronet's hymn appeared in the *Gospel Magazine* for 1779, to-gether with the tune *Miles Lane* by a former chorister of Canterbury Cathedral, Edward Shrubsole, a tune which generations have indissolubly linked with this magnificent hymn. Edward Elgar is said to have pro-nounced the tune the finest in English hymnody.

Perronet's hymn so splendidly affirms the "crown rights" of Christ over all life, and makes a triumphant proclamation of the claims of Christ the King.

Separated though he was from the church of his boy-hood, Edward Perronet was buried in the cloisters of Canterbury Cathedral, not far from his native valley.

BLEST BE THE TIE THAT BINDS

John Fawcett

Round this hymn lies the story of John Fawcett and a company of Baptists in the valley of the Yorkshire river Calder in the middle of the eighteenth century. The Calder was lovelier then than it is now, for the tide of mill buildings, steam engines and the use of Calder's waters for driving the mills had not smeared its beauty. But where Hebden Water joins the Calder the little town of Hebden Bridge stood and not far from it the village of Wainsgate with its Baptist chapel.

One day in 1772 a waggon stood outside the house of the Baptist minister—John Fawcett—loaded up with his goods and chattels. All the village knew that the young minister, at thirty-two, had received an important "call" to a London church, and was about to take the long road south away from his native hills and moors and the people who loved him. He had accepted the invitation, had preached his farewell sermon and had now come to the moment of the last farewell. Many of his congregation stood by the waggon in tears. The sight of so many tearful people, and all the sad hand-shaking he endured, proved too much for John Fawcett. He went back into the house and gave orders to unload the waggon. He had decided to stay amongst his own people and turn his back on the great church he had been asked to minister to under the shadow of St. Paul's Cathedral.

Five years later his people built a splendid new chapel in Hebden Bridge and John Fawcett stayed amongst them for the rest of his life, refusing an invitation in 1793 to be President of the Bristol Baptist Academy. That was the spirit of the man who wrote this tender hymn of affection *Blest be the tie that binds*. He lived the part.

CROWN HIM WITH MANY CROWNS

Matthew Bridges
Godfrey Thring

IT is not surprising that such a magnificent opening line as *Crown him with many crowns* should be used by different hymn-writers. But it is not known whether the two writers of this hymn ever met. Matthew Bridges was one of the considerable group of Anglicans who were influenced by Newman and Faber, and eventually entered the Church of Rome. Godfrey Thring, a much younger man, became a Prebendary of Wells Cathedral in 1876, and it was he who altered and rearranged Bridges' hymn so that both their names now go with it in the hymn-books.

But even good first lines are not always fashioned straight away. The first line of this great hymn used to be *Crown him with crowns of gold*—a line that was for many years popular in the United States, being considered more impressive than any other description.

The five verses celebrate the kingship of Christ each with a definite theme,

> Crown Him the *Lord of Love*
> Crown Him the *Son of God*
> Crown Him the *Lord of Life*
> Crown Him the *Lord of Peace*
> Crown Him the *Lord of Heaven*

thus making the hymn a fine example of Christian teaching about the person of Christ.

FIERCE RAGED THE TEMPEST

Godfrey Thring

HYMNS about the sea seem to make a special appeal to those who speak English. It may be because of the close association of the Anglo-Saxon race with seafaring and its risks. No place in the British Isles is more than a hundred miles from the sea and so the life of fisherfolk means much to those who live in Britain, and this may also be a reason why Galilee, its lake and fishermen have always had their special place.

But this hymn is Australia's choice, a continental island which is also aware of the sea. Oddly enough the great hymn about the sea, *Eternal Father strong to save*, does not appear in the popular choices. Continental people in North America perhaps are not "sea minded" enough to demand it.

I remember being on board the *Queen Elizabeth* in 1944 coming from the United States with many thousands of G.I.s ready for the invasion of France. On the Sunday we assembled for morning worship, and the British Chaplain tried to get the men to sing *Eternal Father*. They didn't know it. Afterwards it dawned on the chaplain that few of those American boys had ever seen the sea before, and hymns about it were unfamiliar. "Give it to British boys," he said, "and they'll sing the roof off."

But in this hymn Godfrey Thring associates Jesus with the storm on Galilee. It is His experience that makes it so singable and real even to landsmen.

GLORIOUS THINGS OF THEE ARE SPOKEN
HOW SWEET THE NAME OF JESUS SOUNDS

John Newton

JOHN NEWTON, Clerk,
Once an infidel and libertine;
A servant of slaves in Africa:
Was by the rich mercy of our Lord and Saviour
Jesus Christ,
Preserved, restored, pardoned,
And appointed to preach the Faith
He had long laboured to destroy.
Near sixteen years at Olney in Bucks,
And twenty-seven years in this Church.

THAT inscription is in the Church of St. Mary Wool-noth, in the City of London, and it sums up the life of the man who wrote these two hymns—one on the Church and one on Jesus, the two poles round which the life of John Newton revolved. Son of a master-mariner, at the age of eleven in 1736 John was a sailor in his father's ship, a happy-go-lucky boy, too, falling early in love with Mary Catlett which never abated "a single moment in my heart from that hour".

He lost his ship, and he even lost it again when he was a midshipman in the navy. Publicly flogged and de-graded for the offence, he managed to get to the African coast and took service under a slave-dealer, whose negro wife cruelly ill-used him. He taught himself Latin, drew triangles of Euclid on the sands of the African shore, read St. Thomas à Kempis and eventually be-came master himself of a slave-ship.

He was a merciful slave captain, coming through shipwreck and storm with some regard for his human cargoes, and gradually, through his study of the Scrip-tures, realizing that this human trafficking was un-

Christian. And so at forty he decided to become an evangelical clergyman, and, with his Mary, settled in as curate at Olney in Buckinghamshire in 1764, where three years later William Cowper also came to live and gave the little town its own special niche in the history of English poetry. There John Newton preached, wrote his hymns, guided the sad, depressed Cowper and then went away to London in 1780 where his bold and burly presence, downright speech, and warm heart drew the City but did not always please its potentates.

If ever there was a "twice-born" man it was John Newton. He was certain of his faith: it had all happened to him,

> Saviour, if of Zion's city,
>   I, through grace, a member am,
> Let the world deride or pity,
>   I will glory in Thy name.

Sometimes it made him very narrow and harsh in his judgments. He once preached a series of sermons in London against Handel's use of the Scriptures in writing the *Messiah*. He called it an entertainment. But underneath the stern exterior Newton had a heart of sympathy and compassion. "Tell me," he once said in a protest against death-bed repentances, "tell me not how the man died, but how he lived." No one but a man who knew religion at first hand could have written *How sweet the name of Jesus sounds* with that haunting fourth verse,

> Jesus, my shepherd, guardian, friend,
>   My prophet, priest, and king,
> My lord, my life, my way, my end,
>   Accept the praise I bring.

Simple, direct and Christian. That was John Newton, and that is why his hymns live. For twenty-seven years the busy life of London stopped to listen to Newton. But in 1893 Newton and his wife were re-buried at Olney, and there they rest by the slow, silent Ouse, where Newton first sang of the "dear name, the rock on which I build".

> Weak is the effort of my heart,
>   And cold my warmest thought;
> But when I see Thee as Thou art,
>   I'll praise Thee as I ought.
>
> Till then I would Thy love proclaim
>   With every fleeting breath;
> And may the music of Thy name
>   Refresh my soul in death.

Newton's hymn glows with the warm, confident experience of the gospel which is personal and triumphant. How could it be otherwise in a life such as Newton's? Often said to be "exclusively emotional", the belief which Newton poured into this hymn was based on historic fact. What Jesus had done He had done for *him*: a fact which Newton celebrates in another hymn,

> One there is above all others
>   Well deserves the name of Friend,
> His is love beyond a brothers,'
>   Costly, free, and knows no end:
> They who once His kindness prove
> Find it everlasting love.

I HEARD THE VOICE OF JESUS SAY

Horatius Bonar

SCOTLAND once had three very famous ministers, the brothers Bonar—John, Horatius and Andrew. In the eighties of the last century their fame as pastors and preachers was amongst the glories of the Scottish churches. Scores of young Scots were named after them. So much did men respect them that on the day Andrew Bonar died a member of his congregation walking down a Glasgow street saw the news-bill, "Death of Andrew Bonar", and felt that for him the end of the world had come. The main prop and stay of his life had, he was sure, departed.

Going on down the street the depressed elder saw two small boys in a perambulator. Their nurse was scolding them. "Look here, Sandy," she said, "sit up, sit up; don't keep leaning on Andrew Bonar!"

It might have been said of Horatius too. A generation and more of Scots leaned on him and his writings. For thirty years Horatius Bonar was a minister in Kelso on the border between Scotland and England, and then worked for another thirty years in Edinburgh until he was past eighty.

Horatius Bonar was a propagandist parson of the best sort at the right time. One of his tracts published in 1839 sold a million copies, and Queen Victoria loved its title, *Believe and Live*. From all over the world people wrote to him about themselves, and out of all this wealth of human contacts came the hymn *I heard the voice of Jesus say*. It is the kind of hymn that arises only out of a pastor's life as he visits and listens, and Bonar had the gift of putting his experiences into little rhymes which were remembered:

Think truly, and thy thoughts shall the world's famine
    feed;
Speak truly, and each word of thine shall be a fruitful
    seed;
Live truly, and thy life shall be a great and noble creed.

The three verses of *I heard the voice of Jesus say* are a
fine example of a pastoral hymn. It is the product of a
working minister amongst his congregation as they
together face the experiences of life:

> I heard the voice of Jesus say,
>   "I am this dark world's light;
> Look unto Me, thy morn shall rise,
>   And all thy day be bright."
> I looked to Jesus, and I found
>   In Him my star, my sun;
> And in that light of life I'll walk
>   Till travelling days are done.

I NEED THEE EVERY HOUR

Annie Sherwood Hawks

A POPULAR hymn and a popular tune came together
one day in April 1872 in Brooklyn, and began a partnership that is unbreakable,

> I need Thee every hour, most gracious Lord;
> No tender voice like Thine can peace afford.

Annie S. Hawks' simple words ask for a simple, memorable melody. They were given it in the twinkling of an
eye by her pastor, Robert Lowry. America first sang
the hymn at conventions and camp meetings, for
Robert Lowry had a sure gift for hymn tunes. His
gospel song books with the titles *Bright Jewels* and *Pure
Gold* had the sentimental and catchy tunes that a huge
crowd loves. Lowry knew his audience and he was
proud of sentimental choruses such as *Shall we gather at
the River?* and *Where is my wandering boy to-night?*

So when Annie S. Hawks, a member of his congregation, came along on the April day in 1872 with the words
of *I need Thee* Lowry saw another opportunity. This
hymn has sung itself into the orthodox hymn-books by
its own simple merits of sincerity in words and tune
alike.

IN CHRIST THERE IS NO EAST OR WEST

John Oxenham

ON a warm London afternoon, June 4, 1908, a slim, eager faced young man in his thirty-fifth year wearing the grey frock coat of a politician in summer dress arrived at a hall in north London to address a meeting. It was more than a meeting. This young member of the government of the day, already in the cabinet as President of the Board of Trade, had come to open a missionary exhibition called the "Orient in London". Over six thousand people were in the great Agricultural Hall, hundreds of them in the costumes of the East. After the singing of the *Old Hundredth* the chairman introduced Mr. Winston Churchill, and the audience listened to a gem of Churchillian oratory, an early example of the speeches which thirty-two years later were to thrill and enhearten the entire free world.

Telling his audience to look beyond the narrow boundaries of their own lives Mr. Churchill said:

> You know very well what a sense of relief it is to us all, as individuals, men and women, when we escape for only a time, perhaps, from the poor little vessel of our own personality, mocked by the deep unseen tides and currents of the ocean—the sport of all the winds that blow; when we can escape from that and take our stand upon some hill-top of high purpose, upon the rock of some great cause, and from that secure position contemplate in serene, yet reverent, independence range upon range of moral or spiritual conception, opening ever more broadly and ever more brightly to the eye of science, of reason and of faith.

Later that day a great pageant of "Darkness and Light" was performed in the hall as part of the exhibition, which Mr. Churchill opened, written by John

Oxenham with music by Hamish MacCunn. One day MacCunn sent hurriedly to Oxenham asking for a few verses to fill a gap in the pageant, and Oxenham wrote these simple lines of genuine belief in the universality of Christ which have won a place in many hymn-books. Oxenham, whose real name was Dunkerley, wrote many novels, and his gift of simple versification comforted millions in the First World War when his little collections of poems, such as *Bees in Amber*, had a wide circulation. John Oxenham was born in 1852 and died in 1941.

The hymn was sung at the opening worship of the Second Assembly of the World Council of Churches at Evanston, U.S.A., on August 15, 1954. Its first line "in Christ there is no east or west" was a most apt proclamation at a time of east-west tensions. Its last verse is a confident assertion of the world commonwealth in Christ,

> In Christ now meet both East and West,
> In Him meet South and North;
> All Christly souls are one in Him,
> Throughout the whole wide earth.

IN THE GARDEN

C. Austin Miles

AMONGST the "gospel song" hymns *In the Garden* holds second place to *The Old Rugged Cross*, and the story of its origin goes back to 1912 when Austin Miles was asked to write a hymn-poem that would be "sympathetic in tone, breathing tenderness in every line; one that would bring hope to the hopeless, rest for the weary, and downy pillows to dying beds".

Miles turned to the Garden of the Resurrection, the first day of the week and Mary Magdalene coming early "while it was yet dark" to the sepulchre.

> I come to the garden alone
> While the dew is still on the roses;
>   And the voice I hear,
>   Falling on my ear
> The Son of God discloses.
>
> And He walks with me, and He talks with me
>   And He tells me I am His own,
> And the joy we share as we tarry there,
>   None other has ever known.

Austin Miles wrote not only the words of his appealing song but the music too, and its popularity is testimony to the fragrance of its memories and its tenderhearted atmosphere. The author was born in 1868 in Lakehurst, N.J., and began his musical career at twelve by playing for a funeral in a rural Methodist church. He played a "slow march", the only one he knew, and he was commended by the preacher and the mourners, and he made his mother proud to hear her boy play so well. He did not know the name of the piece, but learned later that it was the Wedding March from *Lohengrin*! Miles was also a publisher of hymns, and edited scores of hymnals. He died in 1946.

JERUSALEM THE GOLDEN

Bernard of Cluny

MANY hymns come from much longer poems. This one
Bernard wrote in his long thousand-line poem inspired
by the Revelation of St. John. He wrote the poem
De Contemptu Mundi in 1145 and much of it is taken up
with condemning the corruption of the times he lived in.
But that master-translator J. M. Neale (*see* p. 72) spotted
the lovely, majestic lines which celebrate Bernard's
vision of the "heavenly country" and take the believer's
hope forward to the city "whose maker is God".

This hymn is pure poetry. Much of it is decoration
and imaginative description but it expresses the inborn
desire of every believer to be sure that he is a pilgrim to
another country. What Bunyan did for his day Bernard
did for his, and how fortunate we are that we can sing
hymns from both of them—one the abbot of the most
magnificent abbey of France, and the other the singing-
tinker of England. Very different men to meet, but how
alike in their hopes and dreams.

> O mine, O Golden Zion!
> O lovelier far than gold,
> O sweet and blessed country,
> Shall I thy joys behold?
> Jesu, in mercy bring us
> To that dear land of rest,
> Where Thou art with the Father
> And Spirit ever blest.

JESUS LIVES, THY TERRORS NOW

Christian Gellert

IN the choices of British radio audiences this hymn by a German writer ranks very high indeed. In fact it stands with *Jesus shall Reign,* and only one point behind *Jesus Lover.* The hymn-books, of course, put it in the section of the Resurrection and Ascension and it seems to be one of the two hymns (*see* p. 148) of witness to the Resurrection that have been picked out in this way. Gellert was a professor in philosophy at Leipzig from 1751 to his death in 1769, and had two later famous men amongst his pupils, Goethe and Lessing. His calm philosophical approach is seen in this hymn. Compare it with the triumphant note in Charles Wesley's *Christ the Lord is Risen To-day.*

Gellert has been described as a hymn-writer of "rational piety and good taste". But he spoke too for the ordinary man's belief, and his four lines,

> Jesus lives! henceforth is death
> But the gate of life immortal;
> This shall calm our trembling breath,
> When we pass its gloomy portal

say very simply what the Christian believes about death, although it lacks the thrill of Wesley's

> Soar we now where Christ hath led.

Perhaps its very ordinariness accounts for its popularity.

JESUS LOVER OF MY SOUL
LOVE DIVINE ALL LOVES EXCELLING
O FOR A THOUSAND TONGUES
O THOU WHO CAMEST FROM ABOVE
YE SERVANTS OF GOD

Charles Wesley

OUT of the many thousands of hymns that Charles Wesley wrote these five have some claim to stand amongst his greatest, and to have had them chosen by popular choice shows how sound and shrewd a popular choice can be. These five hymns have sung their way into eminence because, to quote Mr. Bernard Manning's *The Hymns of Wesley and Watts* (p. 47) Wesley "is obsessed with the greatest things, and he confirms our faith because he shows us these above all the immediate, local, fashionable problems and objections to the faith. We move to the serener air. We sit in the heavenly places with Christ Jesus; and simply to be taken there— that is, after all, the supreme confirmation of faith."

Charles Wesley seemed to be able to write a hymn almost anywhere and at any time. He wrote five while he was contemplating marriage in 1749, and on other occasions—earthquake, invasion rumours, riots, deaths —he seemed to turn with a natural ease to hymn-writing.

His greatest hymn without doubt is *Jesus Lover*. It has the experience, the doctrine and that sense of universal love which marked the Methodist revival of religion. Round it have clustered many stories, most of them— as far as Charles Wesley himself is concerned—untrue. Although "the nearer waters" and "the tempest high" suggest a storm at sea it is Wesley's poetic imagination at work rather than a direct reference to a particular storm.

But there is one story of the great hymn which has all the signs of a true story about it. It happened that one summer evening in 1881 a party of tourists from the northern United States was enjoying a trip down the Potomac River from Washington. One of the party had a fine voice and began singing hymns to the others. After he had sung two verses of *Jesus, lover of my soul* a stranger came up to him from another part of the steamer and said, "Beg your pardon, sir, but were you in the fighting forces in the late war?" "Yes," said the singer, "I fought under General Grant." "Well, I fought on the side of the South," replied the stranger, "but I believe I was very near you one bright night eighteen years ago this month. If I am not mistaken you were on guard duty that night, and I crept near you with a rifle in my hand. As you paced to and fro you were singing that same hymn, *Jesus Lover*. I raised my rifle and aimed, and at that moment you sang,

> Cover my defenceless head
> With the shadow of thy wing.

I couldn't fire after that, and no attack was made on your camp." The two men gripped hands and the singer said, "I remember the night very well. I was depressed when I went out to duty. I knew it was a dangerous post. As I paced up and down I thought of home and friends, and the thought of God's care, too, came to me so I sang *Jesus Lover*. I never knew until to-night how my prayer was answered."

In Westminster Abbey, London, there is a medallion relief of John and Charles Wesley. Seen in profile the two brothers are most appropriately linked—John the theologian of the Methodist movement and Charles the poet and singer.

In their hymn-book, too, the characteristic liveliness,

point and urgency of the Methodist experience comes out. What John Wesley called "proper heads" includes "Believers Rejoicing, Fighting, Praying, Watching, Working, Suffering, Seeking for Full Redemption, Saved, Interceding for the World". Under those orders Charles soared away in such a hymn as

> Love divine, all loves excelling,
>   Joy of heaven, to earth come down,
> Fix in us thy humble dwelling,
>   All thy faithful mercies crown.

Charles had the light and lovely touch of the lyric writer, but he was also firm and practical in his phraseology—"fix in us", "finish then", "visit us", "suddenly return". These are confident directions which spring from the heart of sure belief.

Charles Wesley wrote the hymn *O for a thousand tongues to sing* to commemorate the anniversary of his conversion of 1738, and the first line probably grew out of a remark by Peter Bohler, one of the Moravian leaders who influenced the Wesleys, who said to Charles, "Had I a thousand tongues, I would praise Him with them all." It is not out of place to note that since Wesley's day the Bible has been translated into "a thousand tongues" and that the great hymn itself has spurred on missionaries and translators in their job.

In fact Charles Wesley was a missionary hymn-writer all the time. He did not write in the first place for church-goers, or for the round of the Christian Year. His eye and pen were on the unconverted. He was out for results—one reason why his hymns are so personal and practical. He also gloried in the belief that God's love was for all men. In *Ye Servants of God* there is the characteristic Wesley "all" running through the hymn,

> Salvation to God,
> > Who sits on the throne!
> Let *all* cry aloud,
> > And honour the Son.

Particularly in the last verse the crescendo of "all" is used with rising and majestic power.

The mark of true religion for the Wesleys was fire and wherever the flame spread it burned up a lot of rubbish, and purified the channels of the faith. One is always amazed at the capacity of Charles Wesley to bring in such a long and difficult word as "inextinguishable" in his hymn *O Thou who camest from above*. The word occupies almost a line to itself,

> There let it for Thy glory burn
> > With inextinguishable blaze;
> And trembling to its source return,
> > In humble prayer and fervent praise.

He handles words with all the sureness of a master, but it is not "sacred poetry" that Charles Wesley writes. As Mr. Manning says, in the book already quoted from, "Why do Wesley's hymns confirm and restore our confidence, and build us up securely in our most holy faith? It is no doubt partly because they show us something of the life of one of the pure in heart who saw God. We may not see God. We cannot fail to see that Wesley saw Him. . . . Purity of heart is inevitably reflected in his clear and limpid verse".

JESUS SHALL REIGN WHERE'ER THE SUN
WHEN I SURVEY THE WONDROUS CROSS

Isaac Watts

ONE May evening in 1944, as World War II reached its climax, I sat with a group of young church people on the southern rim of the Grand Canyon of the Colorado. The deep purples, blues and yellows of fading light were filling the vast abyss of the Canyon with colourful cloud. Here and there a peak stood out above the haze, and as we gazed at the scene stupendous shafts of golden light flashed, and streamed through it all. At one moment two beams of light crossed one another, and for a moment lay fixed and radiant across the width of the Canyon linking the two distant rims, and throwing light into the whirl of cloud and colour below. For a moment we were fixed in silence at the sight, and then spontaneously broke into *When I survey the wondrous Cross*.

That is how Isaac Watts himself would have liked it to be. This little, modest, scholarly man who lived a quiet life at Newington Green on the northern edge of London, and died there in 1748, has a bust in Westminster Abbey but his hymns are the world's. These two in particular celebrate what may be called "the world-lordship" of Christ. Watts was aware of the heavens, the sea, the "realm of nature". What a hymn he would have written after seeing the Grand Canyon! But could he have written anything finer than:

> Forbid it, Lord, that I should boast
>   Save in the death of Christ my God;
>   All the vain things that charm me most,
>   I sacrifice them to His blood.

And yet the hymn does not appear high amongst the popular choices of radio audiences. It is not included in the British list, nor in the Australian, nor the United States. Canada includes it however.

But Watts' greatest hymn is not dependent upon popular choice for its place. It celebrates the foundation of the Christian faith and there has its unique position.

The fame that Queen Salote of Tonga gathered at the time of the Coronation of Queen Elizabeth was a very happy salute to a great lady who rules over an island people which ever since 1862 have been Christian. How they became Christian has a link with *Jesus Shall Reign*. A message was sent by canoe from Tonga to Fiji saying that the Tongans would like to hear about the white man's religion. The reply was a Bible and a missionary, and the result a mass movement on Tonga led by the native monarch King George—Queen Salote's ancestor.

Surrounded by his chiefs and warriors, many of whom had been cannibals, the king formally declared his island kingdom to be Christian, and then the whole multitude broke into *Jesus shall reign where'er the sun* which had been translated into their own Tongan language. No hymn could have been more fitting than this one. This hymn, however, although it has been adopted by "the foreign missionary" movement, rightly stands in any hymn-book under the heading "The Lord Jesus Christ". Watts took Psalm 72 and used the Psalmist's celebration of the "dominion of the Lord" as his celebration of the Kingdom of Christ,

> His kingdom stretch from shore to shore,
> Till moons shall wax and wane no more.

It is all there in the Psalm, but how much more singable in Watts' great hymn. The hymn was one of the four sung at the Opening Service of the Assembly of the World Council of Churches in 1954.

JESUS THOU JOY OF LOVING HEARTS
JESUS THE VERY THOUGHT OF THEE

Bernard of Clairvaux (?)

HYMNS often raise odd associations in the mind. These two, which many authorities are now hesitant to say were written by the great monk Bernard of Clairvaux, always take me to the green, mountainous country beyond Grenoble in France where to-day the traveller is able to go by bus to the great monastery of La Grande Chartreuse. Its secluded position in the mountains makes it a remote spot even to-day, but nothing to what it was in the spring of 1125 when Bernard came riding up the ravines to visit it.

Bernard's letters had already made him famous, but his hosts were disappointed to see him riding such a splendid horse and sitting on so fine a saddle. It was all out of keeping with strict monkish ways. Finally it was mentioned to Bernard, who was surprised at the criticism. Although he had ridden miles on it he had not noticed, he said, how fine the saddle was, and in any case the horse was not his: it had been lent to him for the journey by his uncle!

The monks were happy again, and marvelled at Bernard's deep contemplation which had hidden from him what they saw at first glance. He was later riding by the lake of Geneva, and his companion asked him what he thought of the lake. "What lake?" asked Bernard.

Whether this great man of the twelfth century wrote these lovely hymns to Jesus or no, his character and devotion make him a worthy possibility. No one in Christian history was more deeply devoted to Jesus in every thought and action than Bernard of Clairvaux.

Seven centuries afterwards David Livingstone wrote in his African journal, "The hymn of St. Bernard on the name of Christ pleases me so; it rings in my ears as I wander across the wide, wide wilderness."

The two hymns are from that great quarry *Jesu dulcis memoria*—"the sweetest and most evangelical hymn in the Middle Ages"—whose stanzas laud the Person and Love of Jesus.

Another well-known excerpt from it is *O Jesus, King most wonderful*. How well matched is this hymn of the Middle Ages with the hymns six hundred years later which grew out of the Evangelical Revival.

Here is, it may be, St. Bernard,

> Jesus, the very thought of Thee
> With sweetness fills the breast;
> But sweeter far Thy face to see,
> And in Thy presence rest,

and here is John Newton,

> It makes the wounded spirit whole,
> And calms the troubled breast:
> 'Tis manna to the hungry soul,
> And to the weary, rest.

LEAD ON O KING ETERNAL

Ernest Warburton Shurtleff

THIS fine hymn for youth seems to be born, bred and sung only in the United States. It was written by a young man for his class when they were all on the eve of leaving college to enter the ministry. It was the 1887 class at Andover Seminary, and the young minister-to-be left soon afterwards for his first pastorate at Ventura, Cal. He later ministered at Plymouth, Mass., and Minneapolis, Minn., and then in Europe at Frankfort, Germany, and among American students in Paris.

> Lead on, O King Eternal,
>   The day of march has come;
> Henceforth in fields of conquest
>   Thy tents shall be our home.
> Through days of preparation
>   Thy grace has made us strong,
> And now O King Eternal,
>   We lift our battle song.

It was a grand send-off for that class and has been to countless others at Commencement days and baccalaureate services.

O SACRED HEAD SORE WOUNDED

Paul Gerhardt

WHENEVER this hymn is sung my memory goes back to a Lutheran church in the city of Bielefeld in Germany, and a crowded congregation. The church was so full that people sat round the communion table above which hung a crucifix as large and realistic as any in a Roman Catholic church. The preacher was a pastor who had been imprisoned in Russia and as he told his story, and then came down from the pulpit to stand with the people under the cross and pronounce the Benediction, it seemed as if the great head hanging on the cross bent even lower in sorrow and blessing.

Gerhardt was almost as powerful as Luther himself in interpreting the inner soul of the German people. This hymn does it too. Gerhardt lived through one of the most gloomy times, the Thirty Years' War when his country was torn in religious rivalry. His student life was passed in Luther's own city of Wittenberg from 1628 to 1642, and he was a minister in Berlin and Lubben.

He never had a settled home until he was forty-four; his wife and children all died in early life, and his later years up to his death in 1676 were lonely and gloomy. Most of his hymns begin with the personal pronoun "I" as if in writing them he found relief for his spirit. They all have that deep personal piety of German religion at its best,

> O make me Thine for ever,
> And should I fainting be,
> Lord, let me never, never
> Outlive my love to Thee.

OUR BLEST REDEEMER ERE HE BREATHED

Harriet Auber

THE little town of Hoddesdon lies on the main road from London to Cambridge, not so quiet or secluded now as it was in the days when Harriet Auber lived there. She wrote many hymns in her home there, but like so many hymn-writers she is remembered by one only, this beautiful and timeless lyric.

The story goes that the hymn had an interesting beginning. After church one Sunday she was meditating on the sermon she had heard, as she sat in her bedroom window. Suddenly there came into her mind the first line, "Our blest Redeemer ere he breathed". With her diamond ring she scratched the line, and then the whole verse, on the window pane nearest her.

For years the pane remained in its place, but the Auber home was sold and demolished after Harriet Auber's death.

The seven verses of her hymn have become part of Whitsuntide in the English speaking world. They have that true marriage of Scriptural truth and personal experience which make a Christian hymn,

> He came sweet influence to impart,
>   A gracious, willing guest,
> While He can find one humble heart
>   Wherein to rest.
>
> And every virtue we possess,
>   And every victory won,
> And every thought of holiness
>   Are His alone.

ROCK OF AGES

A. M. Toplady

No hymn has had more romance thrown round it than *Rock of Ages*. According to tradition Toplady when curate of Blagdon in Somerset sheltered from a storm in Burrington Combe, and the shelter was a great cleft in a rock which is there for all to see. It is a likely and lovely story but the facts hardly give it foundation.

Toplady was curate in the parish from 1762 to 1764. His poem, however, did not appear in the *Gospel Magazine* until twelve years later in 1776, and was then used as an argument against John Wesley's doctrine of absolute holiness in man. The idea of Toplady writing the hymn as a thanksgiving for deliverance from a thunderstorm did not, it seems, start up until 1850 when an ingenious vicar of Blagdon spread the rumour.

But, storm or no storm, Toplady's hymn has gone round the world as one of the great evangelical hymns. Long may the "rock of ages" in Burrington Combe be pointed out to visitors as a possible source of Toplady's inspiration, but the "rock" of the hymn "cleft for me" is the Jesus who is both Saviour and Judge.

> While I draw this fleeting breath,
> When mine eyes shall close in death,
> When I soar through tracts unknown,
> See Thee on Thy judgment-throne;
> Rock of ages, cleft for me.
> Let me hide myself in Thee.

SOFTLY AND TENDERLY JESUS IS CALLING

Will Thompson

WILL THOMPSON came out of the state of Ohio where his birthplace was East Liverpool. His musical gifts took him eastwards to Boston and its Conservatory of Music, and two of his songs won more than local fame. But Thompson's heart was in melodies linked to Christian words, and with *Softly and Tenderly* he made a memorable contribution to the revival songs of America at a time when D. L. Moody was leading his evangelistic campaigns.

> Softly and tenderly Jesus is calling
> Calling for you and for me,
> See, on the portals He's waiting and watching,
> Watching for you and for me.

Moody loved this hymn-melody so much that he told Thompson as he lay dying that he would rather have written it than have done anything else,

> Come home, come home,
> Ye who are weary
> Come home.
> Earnestly, tenderly, Jesus is calling,
> Calling, O sinner come home.

Thompson himself died in 1911 at the age of sixty-two.

THE CHURCH'S ONE FOUNDATION

Samuel John Stone

In the sixties of the last century the name of Bishop Colenso of Natal was a name that stood for "heresy" and disloyalty to the basic doctrines of the Christian faith. In a commentary on the Epistle to the Romans, published in 1861, the bishop's treatment of the Atonement and the Sacraments was unorthodox. In fact the bishop himself was unorthodox in many ways. He cared passionately for his Zulu people and their rights and they loved him and gave him the name *Sobantu*, "Father of the People". He even condoned polygamy in certain instances in African life. But when in 1862 he published a critical view of the first five books of the Bible a violent storm burst over his head.

Bishops hurried to condemn his views, and forty of them told him to resign his see. Colenso was practically excommunicated, and when he came to England pulpits were closed against him. The Archbishop of Capetown issued a noble defence of the Christian faith as he saw it and it was this statement which stirred Samuel John Stone, then a curate at Windsor, to write *The Church's One Foundation*.

> Though with a scornful wonder
> Men see her sore opprest,
> By schisms rent asunder,
> By heresies distrest.

Colenso died in 1883 still under a cloud, but the great hymn his "heresies" inspired has become a magnificent statement about the Church. And even some of Colenso's "heresies" are now accepted as a reasonable view of the Scriptures in face of all the later knowledge that God has imparted to scholars. The bishop was before his time, and, perhaps, too hasty in his judgments.

THE OLD RUGGED CROSS

George Bennard

"By a wide margin the top favourite is *The Old Rugged Cross*."

That is the frequent report of the hymn pollsters of the United States.

> On a hill far away stood an old rugged cross
>   The emblem of suffering and shame,
> And I love that old cross where the dearest and best
>   For a world of lost sinners was slain.

That first verse and its companions, and the chorus,

> So I'll cherish the old rugged cross
>   Till my trophies at last I lay down;
> I will cling to the old rugged cross
>   And exchange it some day for a crown

came out of a revival campaign in the small town of Albion, Mich., led by George Bennard, then a Methodist minister. Bennard had been a Salvation Army officer, and knew the power of a swinging melody, a good chorus and words easily memorized.

> To the old rugged cross I will ever be true,
> Its shame and reproach gladly bear,
>   Then He'll call me some day
>   To my home far away
> Where His glory for ever I'll share.

It is simple, evangelical theology and has all the accents of what John Wesley would call "believers believing". There are, of course, some superior people who despise the "gospel song" type of hymn, but there is no mistaking the choice of the people which often passes by accepted orthodoxy in hymns. George Bennard was not far from the heart of sound, emotional religion in *The Old Rugged Cross*.

THERE IS A GREEN HILL
JESUS CALLS US O'ER THE TUMULT

Cecil Frances Alexander

In the middle of the First World War a well-known London doctor was busy one Sunday night in his consulting room. Most of his patients had their illnesses traceable to the war. Worry, anxiety and fear were the principal reasons. As he listened to their explanations the sound of children's voices came floating down the staircase,

> There is a green hill far away,
> Without a city wall.

It was his young family upstairs gathered round his wife at the piano. Leaving his door open and his patients waiting, he rushed up the stairs to join in the hymn. Then coming back he said to his patients, "If we all believed that hymn there would be less worry and less fear."

Mrs. Alexander (*see* p. 29) wrote many of her hymns to teach the Christian catechism. This one is based on the words of the creed, "Suffered under Pontius Pilate, was crucified, dead and buried".

Her other hymn has been changed more than most as successive editors have turned "o'er" into "mid" and back again. Free Church hymn compilers have never cared for "as of old *St. Andrew* heard it" and have gone all out for "*apostles* heard it". That seems to admit that St. Andrew was an Anglican, rather than an apostle of the whole Church.

THOU DIDST LEAVE THY THRONE

Elizabeth Steele Elliott

IF popular choices were expected to include the Christmas hymns some of the "leaders" in popular hymns would probably have strong rivals for first positions. But somehow we find it rather incongruous to sing *Hark the Herald Angels* in midsummer. But not so with Elizabeth Elliott's hymn, which always finds its place amongst Advent hymns in the books.

This hymn, sung at all seasons, is a reminder of the debt all hymn-lovers owe to the women writers of the nineteenth century who found an outlet for their verses in the periodicals and papers associated with the churches and the missionary societies. Miss Elliott, for instance, was the editor of a little magazine called *The Church Missionary Juvenile Instructor* and wrote scores of poems for it. Hardly any of them have survived, except this one which is pure gold, and brings Christmas most happily into all the seasons of the Christian year. But as a sound celebration of the Advent, the hymn moves through the life of Christ up to the Cross,

> Thou camest, O Lord,
> With the living word
> That should set Thy people free;
> But, with mocking scorn,
> And with crown of thorn,
> They bore Thee to Calvary:
> O come to my heart, Lord Jesus!
> Thy cross is my only plea

and then has a last triumphant verse beginning,

> When heaven's arches ring,
> And her choirs shall sing,
> At Thy coming to victory.

WE LOVE THE PLACE O GOD

William Bullock

In the middle of the nineteenth century as a young naval officer William Bullock was a member of a survey expedition along the coasts of Newfoundland. While he was map-making, charting and sounding the depths he was also observing the life of the people. Their poor condition, and isolation from the rest of the world, and lack of religious worship and instruction so depressed him that he left the navy and went back to the bleak coasts as a missionary.

On Trinity Bay he built his first little church, and for it he wrote the hymn which has been more often sung at church dedications than any other. Few men get a chance of building a church, and fewer still write the one hymn which fits the occasion.

> It is the house of prayer,
>   Wherein Thy servants meet;
> And Thou, O Lord, art there
>   Thy chosen flock to greet.

WE SING THE PRAISE OF HIM WHO DIED
THE HEAD THAT ONCE WAS CROWNED WITH THORNS

Thomas Kelly

THESE two hymns stand at the top of the list that Ireland has contributed to the wealth of hymnody in the English tongue.

Kelly was a Dublin man of good family and education with all the likelihood of following his father's distinguished career as a lawyer and judge. But the wave of revival caught him in 1792 as a young man of twenty-three, and he began to preach the good news of Jesus. With his friend Rowland Hill from London, a member of a noble family who also could not be stopped from preaching and for whom the great Surrey Chapel was eventually built, Kelly stirred Dublin with his evangelical passion. It was not to the liking of the Archbishop of Dublin, who banned both young men from church pulpits.

Then Thomas Kelly began an independent ministry, building his own churches, preaching in them, writing hymns, giving his wealth to the poor. He was almost a minor combined Irish edition of John and Charles Wesley. He wrote nearly eight hundred hymns, of which these two have gone round the English speaking world.

WHAT A FRIEND WE HAVE IN JESUS

Joseph Scriven

THE gifts of Ireland to the new world in North America have usually been in a flow of invigorating personalities, and one of them was Joseph Scriven. He landed in Canada in 1845 and lived there until his death in 1886.

Scriven carried with him all his life a secret sorrow which made his devotion to Christ all the more intense —the young lady to whom he was engaged was accidentally drowned on the eve of their wedding day. This sorrow turned his mind also towards poetry, and although his friends were not aware of it Scriven wrote verses himself.

To comfort his mother at a time of special sorrow he wrote out the verses of this hymn, the simple but memorable lines which echo the thoughts of so many hearts. The verses were found by Scriven's own bedside when he lay dying, for he had treasured them for his own comfort too.

When he was asked how he, without any known or marked gifts as a poet, had managed to write the verses he replied, "The Lord and I did it between us." Scriven had unlocked the chief secret in the best hymn-writing which is a partnership between the writer and God. Like all the finest in hymn-writing there is a personal experience running all through Scriven's hymn, simple but sincere, and what more does the reader and the hymn-singer require?

YE SONS AND DAUGHTERS OF THE KING

tr. J. M. Neale

THIS lovely Easter Day hymn is one of John Mason Neale's (*see* p. 72) rich discoveries amongst the Latin hymns. Canada includes it amongst her choices, and although the great array of Easter hymns has been excluded from this book, in order not to throw it out of balance, it was thought right to put *O filii et filiae* amongst the hundred hymns.

The hymn is an example of a Scripture chronicle-hymn with people like the young man at the tomb, the Marys and then doubting Thomas recording the resurrection wonder. Its date is very debateable. It might be as early as the thirteenth century but is more likely to be sixteenth or seventeenth. *Songs of Praise* prints the hymn in two parts with *Alleluya* after each of the ten three-line verses. The first verse is:

> Ye sons and daughters of the King,
> Whom heavenly hosts in glory sing,
> To-day the grave hath lost its sting:

and the last:

> Blessed are they that have not seen,
> And yet whose faith hath constant been;
> In life eternal they shall reign:
> > *Alleluya!*

In *Hymns Ancient and Modern* the first line is given as

> O sons and daughters let us sing.

The authorship of the hymn is attributed to Jean Tisserand, a fifteenth-century Franciscan.

5

HYMNS OF CHRISTIAN ACTION

HYMNS OF CHRISTIAN ACTION

THOMAS KEN — *Awake, my soul, and with the sun*
J. S. B. MONSELL — *Fight the good fight*
S. BARING-GOULD — *Onward! Christian soldiers*
W. P. MERRILL — *Rise up O men of God*
CHARLES WESLEY — *Soldiers of Christ arise*
HENRY ALFORD — *Ten thousand times ten thousand*
B. INGEMANN — *Through the night of doubt and sorrow*
JOHN BUNYAN — *Who would true valour see*
ANNIE W. COGHILL — *Work, for the night is coming*

HYMNS OF CHRISTIAN ACTION

THE nine hymns chosen in this section are the hymns that spring to most people's minds when the Christian call to action is sounded. We begin with Thomas Ken's morning hymn, the hymn which seems to have the sun in it from the first word, and we finish with a popular favourite in the "gospel song" tradition, *Work, for the night is coming.*

The Christian life is a twenty-four hour occupation, and no religion has stirred its believers into action as much as Christianity. Whether it is in the missionary outreach of the gospel, the caring for the homeless and the outcast, the serving of the sick, the young and the aged, the call to action is constantly being heard and answered.

The nine hymns do not sound all the notes in the action call of the Christian, but they sound the fundamental ones. It is interesting to note the "soldier" and "pilgrim" metaphors in five of the hymns, and how magnificently they ring out in the call to the Christian to be both a good soldier and faithful pilgrim.

AWAKE, MY SOUL, AND WITH THE SUN

Thomas Ken

ONE of the great sights of England is Longleat House, the home of the Marquis of Bath, deep in a lush Somerset vale not far from Frome.

Like many great houses to-day Longleat is open to public view and amongst its treasures of pictures, furniture and books is the library of Thomas Ken, the saintly bishop who wrote this hymn. For Bishop Ken lived at Longleat with his friends the Bath family for nearly twenty years until his death in 1711.

When he was Bishop of Bath and Wells William III came to the throne. But, strong Protestant though he was, Thomas Ken felt that his oath of allegiance had been sworn to the banished king James II and his heirs, and therefore he could not swear a loyalty oath to the new king installed by Parliament. So he retired and went to live at Longleat and there his room is shown to visitors. Here the saintly Ken wrote his hymns, sang them to his viol and prayed.

All Englishmen respected Thomas Ken's conscience, and although he was pressed again to become a diocesan bishop, even Queen Anne could not persuade him to swear an allegiance which he felt was false. To show her esteem she gave him a pension of £200 a year.

Thomas Ken wrote his two famous morning and evening hymns for the boys of Winchester college in 1674 with the instruction, "be sure to sing the morning and evening hymn in your chamber devoutly". No hymn-book is complete without these two lovely hymns, but evidently the popular choice is the morning hymn.

Thomas Ken himself perhaps liked it the better of the two, for when he was buried in March 1711 in the churchyard of Frome Selwood he asked that he might lie "under the east window of the chancel just at sun-rising".

> Awake, my soul, and with the sun
> Thy daily stage of duty run;
> Shake off dull sloth, and joyful rise
> To pay thy morning sacrifice.
>
> Lord, I my vows to Thee renew;
> Scatter my sins as morning dew;
> Guard my first springs of thought and will,
> And with Thyself my spirit fill.

No hymn more refreshingly radiates a saintly spirit. It seems to hold, too, the sunlight of an English summer morning as Thomas Ken must have seen it lighting the meads of Wessex.

FIGHT THE GOOD FIGHT

John Samuel Bewley Monsell

THE old town of Guildford lies pleasantly on the River
Wey just thirty miles from London on the road to
Portsmouth. Its steep High Street, with Abbot's
Hospital at the top, the swinging tradesmen's signs, and
the air of happy busyness is a favourite photographic
shot for transatlantic visitors. The Town Hall, the
Grammar School, the churches inserted in between,
and, nowadays, the rising of a new cathedral just outside the town all make Guildford what William Cobbett
called "the most happy looking town".

But on April 9, 1875, a tragedy happened in the town
which cast a gloom over happy Guildford. The vicar of
St. Nicholas, J. S. B. Monsell, was inspecting the roof of
his church, which stands guardian at the bottom of the
famous High Street. Reconstruction work was going on,
and the vicar was up amongst the workmen discussing
their work. He missed his footing and fell heavily off
the roof and died from his injuries.

He was a prolific hymn-writer. There are over three
hundred to his name, but *Fight the Good Fight* is the one
that has found its own niche where good hymns are sung.
Its manly, direct verses with the touch of challenge and
achievement in them are a fine memorial to the Guildford vicar.

ONWARD! CHRISTIAN SOLDIERS

Sabine Baring-Gould

IT was a sunny Sunday morning on August 10, 1941. The British battleship *Prince of Wales* was at anchor in the spacious Placentia Bay, Newfoundland, and on her wide quarter-deck a happy crowd of British and American sailors were gathered for church parade. Facing the great camouflaged guns were sitting two famous men—Franklin Roosevelt and Winston Churchill—singing heartily with the sailors,

> Onward! Christian soldiers,
> Marching as to war,
> With the cross of Jesus
> Going on before.

Together the two men had chosen the hymns for this church parade at which the American and British sailors stood shoulder to shoulder, a symbol of what was to come later in the same year.

Churchill's choices were *Our God our help in ages past*, and *Onward Christian soldiers*. Roosevelt pleaded for *Eternal Father strong to save*, too, and so the three great hymns rose through the still morning air at this historic meeting where the Atlantic Charter was signed.

After he returned home across the dangerous ocean waves Churchill broadcast to the British people about the hymn singing:

> We sang *Onward Christian Soldiers* and indeed, I felt that this was no vain presumption but that we had the right to feel that we were serving a cause for the sake of which a trumpet has sounded from on high. When I looked upon that densely packed congregation of fighting men of the same language, of the same faith, of the

same fundamental laws, of the same ideals . . . it swept across me that here was the only hope, but also the sure hope, of saving the world from measureless degradation.

So the hymn which Baring-Gould wrote in 1865 for his Sunday school children to march to in their procession through the village street of Horbury Brig (*see* p. 94) was lifted on this occasion to a marching song for all the free peoples.

The hymn's third verse,

> We are not divided,
>   All one body we,
> One in hope and doctrine,
>   One in charity,

was certainly written with an eye on the Horbury children as they marched in unity and unison. No doubt it was that vision too which inspired Winston Churchill as he looked over the quarter-deck of the *Prince of Wales* on that sunlit morning in 1941 and saw the young sailors of the old and new worlds standing and singing together.

RISE UP O MEN OF GOD

William Pierson Merrill

FOR twenty-seven years from 1911 to 1938 Pierson Merrill was pastor of the famous Brick Presbyterian Church in New York.

He was always interested in the task of presenting the Christian faith to men, and had a large following of men who liked his honest, manly approach to religious problems. The years of his ministry were the years of the Brotherhood movement, and this hymn arose out of the author's link with it.

One day in 1911 he was crossing Lake Michigan, and as he sat on the steamer's deck the hymn formed itself in his mind. "It came to me quite without effort or forethought," he wrote afterwards.

It was a hymn of its own times and carries the stamp of the optimistic days of pre-1914,

> Bring in the day of brotherhood,
> And end the night of wrong.

The hymn, as the last verse shows, does not intend to suggest that man is able to do all by himself, although the hymn is perhaps open to that criticism. But the vigour and challenge of the original lines will always win its singers whatever the changes in the theological climate may be.

SOLDIERS OF CHRIST ARISE

Charles Wesley

HERE is the model hymn of Christian action. It has the martial spirit without worldly boasting, for it is centred in our Lord's achievement as victor over this world, and points the believer to His ultimate triumph,

> From strength to strength go on,
> Wrestle, and fight, and pray,
> Tread all the powers of darkness down,
> And win the well-fought day.
> Still let the Spirit cry
> In all his soldiers, "Come",
> Till Christ the Lord descend from high,
> And take the conquerors home.

Charles Wesley's unmatched gift of rising to a mighty crescendo of affirmation and action is seen in the verses of this hymn. Every line is a challenge, and yet every line is an assurance of the unseen strength available.

> Stand then in His great might,
> With all His strength endued;
> And take, to arm you for the fight,
> The panoply of God;
> That having all things done,
> And all your conflicts passed,
> Ye may o'ercome through Christ alone,
> And stand entire at last.

TEN THOUSAND TIMES TEN THOUSAND

Henry Alford

THE cradle of Christianity for the English speaking peoples is Canterbury, and two hymns which are widely used and loved were first sung in the cathedral at Canterbury when Henry Alford reigned there as Dean from 1857 to 1871. One is *Forward be our watchword*, which the Dean composed as he walked round his cathedral measuring the time that a procession would take. That's why the hymn is so long!

And the other is *Ten Thousand Times*. It is another processional hymn, but perhaps for shorter processions!

> Ten thousand times ten thousand,
>   In sparkling raiment bright,
> The armies of the ransomed saints
>   Throng up the steeps of light;
> 'Tis finished—all is finished—
>   Their fight with death and sin!
> Fling open wide the golden gates,
>   And let the victors in.

Ten Thousand Times has something of the soaring wonder of Canterbury's great nave, "the steeps of light", in it. You can almost see the great procession of the saints passing down the nave and through the gates into the lighted chancel.

THROUGH THE NIGHT OF DOUBT AND SORROW

Bernhardt Ingemann

THIS hymn was a brilliant discovery of Sabine Baring-Gould who no doubt liked its marching tones, and its note of triumph so similar to his own *Onward! Christian Soldiers*.

He found it in a collection of hymns for Danish churches by the poet Bernhardt Ingemann. He translated it for the same children at Horbury in Yorkshire who first marched to and sang *Onward! Christian Soldiers*.

Ingemann himself, who died in 1862, wrote stories for Danish children, and had a reputation amongst them almost as great as Hans Andersen. They loved his tales so much that with their collected half-pennies they bought him a golden horn decorated with figures from his poems and stories.

Ingemann's hymn is another instance of the genuine universality of hymn-writing and hymn-singing. It expresses the "pilgrim" nature of the Christian life, and its four verses which each begin with the word "One" express the unity of Christian purpose. No doubt that also appealed to Baring-Gould, as a reference to page 156 will show. But yet there is a marked difference between the two hymns. Ingemann's hymn has a deeper note all the way through—perhaps a little more theology, and certainly more eschatology. Baring-Gould's own hymn is militant and martial enough, but has it the personal appeal of this one?

WHO WOULD TRUE VALOUR SEE

John Bunyan

BUNYAN is happily amongst the hymn choices of the English speaking people, which is only fit and proper for a master of the English tongue.

Not that Bunyan was a hymn-writer, or even aspired to be one. His pilgrim's song is Mr. Valiant-for-truth's effort, and is a celebration of his triumph over Mr. Fearing and Mr. Despondency. It is his triumph over the avarice of Obstinate and Pliable, Mistrust and Timorous, Turnaway and Old Atheist.

"And did none of these things discourage you?" asked Mr. Greatheart of Valiant-for-Truth.

"No; they seemed but as so many nothings to me."

"How came that about?"

"Why, I still believed what Mr. Tell-true had said, and that carried me beyond all," said Valiant-for-truth.

"Then this was your victory, even your faith," said Mr. Greatheart.

"It was so. I believed, and therefore came out, got into the way, fought all that set themselves against me, and, by believing, am come to this place."

> Who would true valour see,
>   Let him come hither;
> One here will constant be,
>   Come wind, come weather;
> There's no discouragement
> Shall make him once relent
> His first avowed intent
>   To be a pilgrim.

WORK, FOR THE NIGHT IS COMING

Annie Walker Coghill

Work, for the night is coming,
   Work through the morning hours;
Work while the dew is sparkling,
   Work 'mid springing flowers;
Work when the day grows brighter,
   Work in the glowing sun;
Work, for the night is coming
When man's work is done.

ANNIE LOUISE WALKER, who was later to marry Harry Coghill, was only eighteen when she wrote the words of this famous gospel hymn. It is based on St. John 9: 4, "The night cometh when no man can work". She was born in England, but later lived in Canada, and it was while in Canada in 1854 that the hymn was written, probably under the sense of the pioneering necessity of work, and more work, which helped to lay the foundations of Canada in the late nineteenth century,

Work till the last beam fadeth,
   Fadeth to shine no more,
Work, while the night is dark'ning
When man's work is o'er.

It is said that she disliked Lowell Mason's setting of her song, but his vigorous music has helped to give *Work, for the night is coming* a firm tread which goes well with the words.

THE HUNDRED HYMNS

First lines

AUTHORS